English coursework

Jeremy Sims is Head of English at
and a Team Leader in GCSE Engl

*English coursework themes
also available in Pan:*

Drama and Poetry
Prose
Conflict
Women and Society

Brodie's Notes on
English coursework
The Short Story

Jeremy Sims

Pan Books London, Sydney and Auckland

First published 1991 by
Pan Books Ltd, Cavaye Place, London SW10 9PG

9 8 7 6 5 4 3 2 1

© Pan Books Ltd 1991

ISBN 0 330 50307 3

Photoset by Parker Typesetting Service, Leicester

Printed in England by Clays Ltd, St Ives plc

This book is sold subject to the condition that it shall not,
by way of trade or otherwise, be lent, re-sold, hired out
or otherwise circulated without the publisher's prior consent
in any form of binding or cover other than that in which
it is published and without a similar condition including this
condition being imposed on the subsequent purchaser

The Short Story

Short Story texts

The short stories referred to in this guide have mostly been taken from the following collections, which are among those commonly recommended by the Examining Boards at GCSE level. Each story discussed is followed by a number that refers you back to the relevant collection. Thus 'Samphire'[2] is to be found in the second collection here, 'Modern Short Stories'.

1 *Twentieth Century Short Stories* Barnes and Egford (ed.) (Nelson 1985)

2 *Modern Short Stories* Jim Hunter (ed.) (Faber 1964)

3 *Selected Tales* D. H. Lawrence, ed. Ian Serraillier (Heinemann Educational 1963)

4 *Caribbean Stories* Michael Marland (ed.) (Longman: Imprint Books 1978)

5 *Late Night on Watling Street* Bill Naughton (Longman: Imprint Books 1969)

6 *My Oedipus Complex and other stories* Frank O'Connor (Penguin 1990)

7 *The Loneliness of the Long-Distance Runner* Alan Sillitoe (Granada: Panther 1985)

8 *Short Stories of our Time* D. R. Barnes (ed.) (Nelson 1985)

9 *Off-Beat* Frank Whitehead (ed.) (Hart-Davis Educational 1979)

Contents

Preface by the general editor viii

Introduction
The appeal of the story 1, The 'modern short story' 2, Structure 4, Viewpoint 7, Style 8, Summary 10

Parents and Children
The significance of a title 12, The importance of the opening sentence 17

A Significant Experience
Turning points 24, Turning points – the consequences 28

The Outsider
Victims 34, The key moment – reported 39, The importance of the setting 42

Living with the consequences
Moments in a life 46, Atmosphere through dialogue 52

The Setting
An industrial landscape 55, Effects of sound and light 57, Unfamiliar backgrounds 58

Humanity and Nature
Unequal struggles 63, A real or imagined struggle? 65, A symbolic struggle 68

Humour
Escaping reality 72, Through the eyes of a child 73

Style
Imagery 80, Simplicity 81, Symbolism 82, Tone of voice 84, Character 86

The Novella
Being honest to yourself 88

Conclusion 95

General questions 98

Questions for wider reading 100

Index of stories discussed in the text 102

Preface

The thematic approach to the study of literature has long been practised by teachers, and this new series of Brodie's Notes focuses on areas of investigation which will help teachers and students at GCSE and A-level alike.

The Notes will stimulate disciplined and imaginative involvement with your chosen books by widening your horizons to the possibility of studying works which are comparable in theme (say, Conflict) or genre (say, the Short Story).

Do not get so absorbed that you see *only* the theme under discussion and nothing else: the theme of any book – whether the presentation of marriage, or of love, or conflict – is only a part of the whole. Read primarily to enjoy and discover, and try to work out how important the theme you are examining is to the whole: it may reside in character or situation or social conditions or any number of areas. One thing is sure: by recognizing and appreciating the theme or themes you will have learned more about the work you are studying. As a result you will be able to write about it more fully, and place it in a broader literary context.

The editor of each Theme/Genre Note in this series is an experienced teacher, and his or her aim is to promote your interest in a range of ideas and books – whether prose, drama or poetry, at the same time extending your capacity for literary appreciation and your imaginative participation in what you read.

For more specific help, you can refer to Brodie's Notes on individual texts.

Graham Handley 1991

Introduction

The appeal of the story

In Maupassant's story 'The Necklace'[9], a woman's life is ruined because she loses the expensive necklace that she has borrowed from a friend. Not admitting the loss, she and her husband borrow money to replace the necklace, and they live in poverty for ten years in order to repay the debt. At the end of ten years she 'now looked an old woman', and she meets her friend by chance in the street. She learns from the friend that the necklace was actually an imitation worth comparatively little.

While little more than an anecdote, the story helps to show the appeal of the short story. We are given a glimpse of characters with whom we become involved – of the hopes and frustrations of Mathilde's life particularly. We are shown her excitement at attending the 'select' party, and then the single moment that destroys her life, the loss of the necklace. We are involved in the 'story' element too – how will the situation be resolved? We can perhaps share her horror at losing something so valuable which has been borrowed.

A further glimpse of the drudgery of her next ten years, as all her hopes are destroyed, sustains our sympathy. The twist at the end brings an ironic and unexpected climax. There is, too, an incompleteness about the short story. Unlike the novel, loose ends are rarely tidied up. The reader's imagination can continue to work. For instance, in 'The Necklace', we remain interested in how the woman will respond to her friend's final comment.

The short story engages our emotions and interest in people. We are involved in what happens – the 'story' itself. The incompleteness is rather like that of life, where we often catch a sight of something that is not resolved. More is suggested in a short story than it ever tells us. Our imagination is always creatively engaged.

This perhaps explains the long history of the story and its popularity in all cultures. With language came the possibility of telling a story, perhaps the telling or developing of a simple anecdote which arrests our attention in some way. Indeed the modern short story is often told in such a way that it suggests someone is talking to us, just as we may tell a friend or relative something that has happened to us or to someone we know. The modern short story emerges from a tradition in which stories were spoken, not read.

The 'modern short story'

When we think of the short story today, however, it is likely that we are thinking of a form that has developed mainly since the middle of the nineteenth century. Whatever it may owe to an oral tradition, this type of short story was designed to be read. It developed partly because of an increase in the number of people who could read.

In England, the nineteenth century was the great age of the novel, and the short story was slower to develop than in America or in Europe. It is to an American short story writer of the early nineteenth century, Edgar Allan Poe, that we might turn for a simple definition of the story. He wrote of a 'short prose narrative requiring from a half-hour to one or two hours in its perusal'. While this may be true of longer short stories or 'novellas' – discussed later – many of the stories considered here can be read in less time. We might revise this definition to: *A short prose narrative that can be read in between ten minutes and an hour and a half.*

Poe saw too that much of the impression that the short story makes relies on its unity – on achieving a single particular effect over a single reading. However limited the story described, or however little we learn of a character, we follow through the situation to a kind of resolution or conclusion. This 'single effect' developed in two main directions. Firstly, in stories concerned with what happens – where the reader's interest is mainly held by the incidents and episodes of the narrative. Secondly, in stories mainly concerned with the reality of a situation by showing us 'ordinary' scenes from life; closer to a painting, we are thrust into a scene with no preparation. We know nothing more of the characters than what we hear them say, or how we see them respond. Some stories of course combine these two approaches.

The first approach relies more on the reader's immersion in the story, and is more likely to introduce the idea of 'a final twist', an unexpected ending. The second approach tends to present scenes apparently from real life – not tidy stories – which by their nature tend not to be dramatic; often, little happens. Both bring with them something of the complexity of real life, but while this second approach reveals how people actually respond in their everyday lives, the first presents the character faced with a predicament which reveals something of his or her personality.

Like a novel, the modern short story always shows us something of how people respond to life. The method of the short story is inevitably more limited than that of the novel. A novel tries to create a world, its own reality, within which its characters develop. In some novels we are apparently shown the 'whole life' of a character. As it is impossible to write about every second of that character's existence, the novelist presents the 'whole life' in a series of moments, key incidents that create a strong sense of the kind of person he or she has invented. In the short story, however, we may catch only a glimpse of individuals – either through a dramatic incident, or by showing them in an everyday situation, or by showing fleeting moments from their lives – from which the reader may gain some but not an entire impression of character.

While we may feel that we really know characters in a novel, and may respond to them as to people in real life, it is rarely possible to feel the same for a character in a short story. Characters in the short story are closer to those people in real life with whom we have fleeting contact, like chance meetings, holiday acquaintances. We share time with them but know little about them, of their past or of what they are really like – and then perhaps lose contact. All that remains is a brief impression based on a few shared moments. Much of the appeal of the short story lies in this incompleteness; it raises questions, doubts, ambiguities.

Usually the short story raises more questions than it answers. It arouses our curiosity. Why do certain characters behave as they do? How have they arrived in the situation? What will they do next? Just as poetry often seeks to communicate feeling or emotion which is often difficult – perhaps impossible – to put into words, so the 'incompleteness' of the story can hint at states of mind or feeling common to us all, but difficult to bring out with clarity. Like a poem, the short story can rely on a kind of 'suggestiveness', for example, where it tries to evoke a mood rather than showing it. It certainly shares some qualities with poetry – it seems no accident that poets like Walter de la Mare, Dylan Thomas and Ted Hughes have also written short stories.

So in general terms, we have at least some starting points for a definition of the short story. Often it is concerned with a single incident, a telling incident, in a person's life. In that character's response to the moment, we learn something about him or her, and in a good story, we might learn something about ourselves. How might we have faced the same situation? How did the situation arise? Could it have been avoided? If the incident was one the character seeks – as Sally Carroll seeks marriage in 'The Ice Palace'[2], or as Leila in 'Her First Ball'[2] excitedly awaits the ball – is the experience what they expected? How does it differ from what they hoped? Were their expectations realistic?

Structure

The short story is often based around a single key moment or incident in the life of the character(s). At times it represents a turning point in a character's life. It can be a moment that actually triggers tension or conflict between two individuals, or an individual and society. It may be less the moment itself than the character's response to it, or its consequences, that interest the writer. In such cases the key moment might already have occurred or been reported. Some moments can be trivial and ordinary; others seem dramatic and quite out of the ordinary.

In 'Shot Actress – Full Story'[8], Sprake's life is completely changed through a single moment. The story relies on its events to engage our initial interest. Sprake, the main character, tells us the story himself. In brief, a mysterious woman is shot; Sprake discovers the body and his account of what he saw is much in demand by the press; as interest in the case wanes, Sprake is left alone again. The 'single incident' here is his discovery of the woman's body. What concerns us however are the consequences of her death on Sprake. He is manipulated by the press, and gradually implicated in her death; his business is ruined, his wife kills herself.

Some short stories may open with an introduction that sketches the main character(s), and perhaps hints at the conflict or tension at the centre of the story. There is sometimes here an initial, less significant incident, which helps us to define the characters involved, often through dialogue, which is an economic means of conveying character. There then may follow the main conflict – the key moment – of the story which brings it to its climax. This can be followed by a resolution – the consequences of the major incident, and sometimes by a conclusion. During the last two stages, resolution and/or conclusion, there is often a 'twist', a sting in the tail that the reader does not expect.

If we consider 'The Lumber Room'[1], the opening two pages present us with the small incident of the frog in Nicholas's bread-and-milk. This enables us to focus on the conflict between Nicholas and his self-styled aunt. It gives us an insight into the strategic skills of Nicholas, and the rather narrow-minded attitudes of his aunt, thus preparing us for the way the story will develop. The major conflict follows over the aunt's certainty that Nicholas wants to enter the forbidden gooseberry garden; in fact, Nicholas uses this conflict to explore the lumber room, which is what he had planned. The resolution comes with the aunt's imprisonment in the rainwater tank, and the possibility for Nicholas to seek revenge. The conclusion considers the failure of the trip organized for the other children, as a means of punishing Nicholas. The narrative interest is sustained through the two 'twists' or surprises: that Nicholas actually wants to visit the lumber room not the gooseberry garden, and the failure of the expedition. Such a summary ignores the humour of the story of course, which will be considered later in this study (see pp. 75–6).

The narrative interest helps to focus our attention on the single, often decisive moment, and what it reveals of the central character. The moment is often one of great tension or conflict and we follow the character through the consequences to some kind of resolution. In some stories, however, we are plunged straight into the incident, and the interest lies in how the situation is resolved. In 'The Dry Rock'[8], Tarloff's cab is involved in an accident almost immediately. It is the reaction of the characters to the accident that interests us. We are particularly concerned with Tarloff's response, for the consequences of the accident bring to a head all he suspects about the nature of American justice. 'A Village Tragedy'[4] also opens with the main incident – the terrible wounds inflicted on Ambrose Beckett by the boar. Our interest then focuses on the responses of key members of his family, and the village, to his subsequent death, responses that seem more self-centred than compassionate.

Sometimes the crucial moment of the short story has already happened before the story begins. The focus of interest becomes how the character deals with the consequences. In Hemingway's 'The Killers'[9], we contrast the reaction of Nick, the eye-witness of the intended murder, and that of the intended victim, Ole Andresen. While Nick decides that he must leave the town, Andresen has come to terms with the inevitable results of his undisclosed act, and stays to face his death. In 'The Daughters of the Late Colonel'[1], the death of the girls' father is used to reveal the extent of the damaging influence he has had upon his daughters.

Often the character involved in this single moment does not grasp the significance of what is happening. The reader may well grasp what the character fails to understand. Readers of 'Uncle Ernest'[8], for example, are made aware of Ernest's appearance, and are in a position to judge the kind of impression he must make when he befriends the two girls; the conclusion of the story may surprise us less than it clearly does Ernest himself. Elsen in 'The Road'[2] seems similarly naïve as he tries to piece together the life he remembered before his ten years at sea. The painful movement towards the reality of the situation is apparent to the reader before Elsen dares face the truth.

The short story can show change in the main character, not through one incident but through several small moments at a significant time in the character's life. While still lacking the space for the full psychological development of the character, this kind of story might look at a period in the character's life, rather than at a specific isolated moment. It might be the series of skirmishes we see in 'My Oedipus Complex'[6], as Larry tries to retain his mother's attention in competition with his father, newly returned from the First World War. Or the series of rather eccentric incidents in which Mr Cronch becomes involved in 'Lie thee down, Oddity'[2], where we see a man leaving a world of safe, conventional values in order to face the challenging decisions of life.

The narrative interest of the short story is often central to its appeal. In some stories, however, we are merely presented with a slice of somebody's life. Nothing 'happens' as such. We are encouraged to focus our attention less on the 'tale', more on the

Introduction

characters and what is revealed of them in ordinary life. In 'The Daughters of the Late Colonel'[1], we see the daughters continuing their normal lives, but in the shadow of their father's death. Through their attitudes to living, we learn a great deal about their father's influence on their past lives, and how their future too is likely to be affected.

Viewpoint

Our attitude to the short story is often influenced by who is telling that story. From whose point of view is the story told? Most commonly, authors write in the third person. Here, the person telling the story often seems to be quite outside the events that make up the story. The narrator seems to know all about the characters, shows us how they act and how they think, and often appears to be neutral towards them – merely showing how they respond in a particular kind of situation; the events are described almost as if through the eyes of a reporter. 'The Wedge-Tailed Eagle'[2], and 'Hunters and Hunted'[4] are written like this.

Sometimes with the third person narrative, we are encouraged to see the story through the eyes of one of the characters. We often identify with this character, and perhaps sympathize with him or her. We might feel caught up in Leila's enthusiasm in 'Her First Ball' or have a certain sympathy with Walter Mitty's life and the escapist fantasies he needs to survive it, in 'The Secret Life of Walter Mitty'[2]. We are made to feel Romesh's struggle in 'Cane is Bitter'[4] between his old world and the possibilities of a new world that education has brought him. At other times, the reader's view is being quietly manipulated by the writer. In 'The Little Pet'[8], it appears that we are being told a story by an author who understands everything about his characters. In fact, while he analyses the parents in the story, we are left to judge little Francis from his rather flat dialogue, and to determine therefore the relationship between the three.

In some cases the story is told in the first person. This can suggest that the story is autobiographical (that it is about the person who is telling the story). 'My Oedipus Complex'[6], for instance, opens with Larry talking about his father: '... up to the age of five, I never saw much of him, and what I saw did not worry me.' 'Peaches'[2] too plunges us into a child's experience told from his point of view. In both cases the child's perspective adds to the humour of the story, the child seeing his world in quite different terms to those of an adult. The first-person narrator in 'Late Night on Watling Street'[5], however, as one of a close-knit community of lorry drivers, reveals himself to be modest, decent, and fair-minded, while understanding the particular pressures facing the drivers. He becomes the ideal witness of an act that breaks their 'code'; his reaction guides ours.

There are limitations in the first-person viewpoint. Everything in the story is seen through the eyes of the 'I' figure. What he cannot see happening cannot be described. Some of the appeal of this approach, however, is that he does not necessarily understand what he hears and reports; or he may misinterpret it. The reader becomes involved though, because he or she may feel closer to such a narrator. The events seem to be happening before him or her, the reader may feel part of the experience. We may share Sprake's growing bewilderment in 'Shot Actress – Full Story'[8], as the media take control and interpret in their own way his innocent act of concern for his neighbour.

Style

Most short stories offer us some insight into character. Many involve us in a 'story', an anecdote or tale. The style of the writer is clearly important too: here 'style' is used in a narrow sense to suggest the way a writer uses language to present his or her story. Coleridge talked of poetry as 'the best words in the best order', and his words seem appropriate enough to define the short story. A writer may rely on descriptive language to establish a precise setting for his story, to evoke a particular place, mood or atmosphere.

In other stories, the title may point us to a telling image or symbol – whereby an idea or feeling which is difficult to express is presented through a comparison with something else felt to have similar qualities. The comparison may help to clarify the concerns of the writer. In Ted Hughes' story 'The Rain Horse'[2], it is often difficult to determine whether the rain horse is real or imaginary. Eventually it seems to be both. A real animal, it is a frightening physical presence. Symbolically, however, it seems also to represent elements of the past, to which the main character thinks he wants to return, but which actually he is reluctant to face. In

'Odour of Chrysanthemums'[1,3] while there are only a few mentions of the chrysanthemums, they represent significant moments in the lives of Elizabeth and Walter Bates which help us to understand Elizabeth's despair at realizing the truth about her relationship with her husband. The red ball in the story of that name represents a sense of acceptance by the boy of his new community. In 'The Dry Rock'[8], the title points us to Tarloff's eventual fate, that of being abandoned on his 'dry rock of principle'.

Some writers use straightforward language to tell a story simply. In stories like 'Shot Actress – Full Story'[8] or 'A Present for a Good Girl'[8] the language seems simple, down-to-earth, to reflect what are ordinary people. The simplicity makes us better able to appreciate the way in which ordinary situations can get out of hand.

In the stories of D. H. Lawrence, the setting is more important – often that of the drab, grimy mining communities of Nottingham. The opening paragraph of 'Odour of Chysanthemums'[1,3] makes the reader quickly aware of the nature of the industrialized landscape, the dominance of the colliery providing the inhabitants both with a living and a gloomy, polluted environment. This setting becomes an important feature of many of Lawrence's stories, as it does too for his novels. Equally, 'Hunters and Hunted'[4] and 'A Village Tragedy'[4] both rely on the way the atmosphere of the rain forest is created.

Another aspect of style to consider is the use of dialogue. Because the short story relies on compression, it tends rather to present than to explain. Instead of describing a tone of voice, or what a person is feeling, the writer may merely include what characters say. Again, this throws the emphasis on the reader's interpretation, thus adding to the sense of ambiguity, so often part of the story's interest. It becomes an economic way of getting across a sense of character. While some of the tension of 'The Raid'[8] is conveyed through the description of the town, more is presented through the edgy, fragmented conversation of Dick and Root; it is through the dialogue that we grasp their dangerous situation, their fear and their courage. In the short 'Blackout'[4], the central conflict revolves around the dialogue that establishes the difference between the two. In 'The Road'[2], much of the story is in dialogue, so the reader can experience the alienation Elsen feels from what used to be his home area, and can hear the way local people try to avoid becoming involved in his problems. It is through making us hear the tone of 'Lacey's' voice in 'Samphire'[2], that the author establishes his wife's contempt and hatred for him.

Summary

With a good short story there are many things which might catch our attention. We might be most involved in the action of the story. We might feel puzzled by the story, intrigued or surprised. We might be more struck by the setting or atmosphere of the story. It might be the nature or behaviour of the characters that we feel drawn to. We might think about the way in which the writer is telling the story:

Are we told about the characters?
Do we have to make up our own minds about character from dialogue?
How much are we told, how much do we have to interpret?

We might be more interested in the story's aim:

What was the writer's intention in producing the story?
Have we perhaps learned something about ourselves?
Do we compare how we might react to similar situations with the response of the characters?

The short story – like all literature – goes beyond itself. Just as a poem reduces experience and tries to collect it perhaps in a short lyrical statement, so the short story reduces life to a few moments, or to just one significant instant, but implies so much more than it tells. We might look to the title or opening sentence of the story to suggest the focus of its interest, but its significance, its meaning, generally goes beyond such limits. The discussion of individual stories which follows here collects stories under general themes, and draws attention to others that might be considered under a similar heading. But there are other themes, other stories, other ways of thinking about the short story that will catch the attention of different people. There is no one way of considering the short story; what follows is intended to offer positive, stimulating, rewarding approaches, together with ideas and assignments on how to discuss and write about stories in various ways. There are creative approaches too, which might encourage you to write your own stories!

Parents and Children

The short story can be concerned with a significant moment of tension or conflict. Such tension is sometimes generated within the family, and the most testing relationship can be that between the parent(s) and child. Often misunderstanding is at the centre of such family problems. The reason why a parent or child behaves in a particular way is not always perceived by the other. The parent might feel that he or she is behaving in the best interests of the child, without considering fully the effects of an action on the child. The child may not be able to see the whole picture, for example the pressures on a parent which can provoke a certain kind of behaviour. Unlike a novel, where a fuller sense of the relationship might eventually become clear, a short story focuses on a moment, often of the greatest tension, to suggest elements of the relationship.

The reader's sympathies are conditioned by the narrative technique. If, say, the child is presented in the first person, we will see the moment through his or her eyes. Much may be revealed about him in the way he tells the story, and his feelings as he does so. If narrated in the third person (where the author writes of 'he' or 'she') – the story's effect will be different. We may feel that we are being told a story by an author who knows everything about his characters – and we need merely make our own judgements. At other times the narrator might guide our response by the way he presents his characters.

In 'The Little Pet'[8] and 'The Red Ball'[4], a triangle of characters is involved: father, mother and child. In both cases the story is told in the third person. 'The Little Pet' appears to be an objective account but in fact the narrative analyses the characters of the parents, while giving only dialogue by which to judge little Francis. In 'The Red Ball', the third-person narrative is more objective, and while we seem initially to view it from Bolan's perspective, all the characters are eventually encompassed – the tension is outside the family, its symptoms within. The title of each story focuses attention on the main issue that creates tension or conflict. In both stories, the parents are apparently trying to do the best for their child, and it is through the child's response to the parents' efforts that we are made to reach judgements about their relationships.

The significance of a title

Parents who try too hard

In 'The Little Pet'[8], Francis and Martha buy little Francis a pet rabbit – apparently for his amusement. Through this seemingly innocuous action, Dan Jacobson begins to reveal the reality of the relationship between the parents and child. Francis and Martha, the parents, are first presented, and we are introduced quickly to their characters; they react to life with the 'strained and guilty air of the perpetually well-intentioned'; they do not respond to life naturally but as they think they ought to act. They find it difficult to show emotion and affection – they both laugh 'a practised, accommodating, nervous laugh' in their attempts at 'meeting each other at all points'.

The focus of the story then switches to little Francis, who does not join their laughter, and responds to their encouragement to enjoy the rabbit with the repeated and neutral 'Yes', denying any child's enthusiasm at the prospect of a new pet. Not discouraged, they 'work' at the fun the rabbit will provide for their son, despite the awkwardness of the hutch and the expense of feeding it out-of-season vegetables.

Despite their talk of 'a bunny', or their ignorant hope for twenty baby 'bunnies', the boy's response seems more realistic and mature than theirs: 'Do rabbits ever have twenty babies?', the distinction between the attitudes being underlined in the words 'bunnies' and 'babies'. They can only present the rabbit in fantasy terms: 'Granny', 'a darling of a bunny brer rabbit' to convince themselves and little Francis of its 'Christmas card' reality. When they register its actual reality, they are fearful of the possibility of its fleas or of its bite. Indeed the appearance of the rabbit is rather disconcerting, described in rather violent terms, 'the almost hammer-like' central bone of the face, the mouth with upper lip 'split so horribly ... gaping like some sort of wound', the tips of some of the hairs 'the colour of dried blood'. This is far from the 'little pet' they anticipated.

The rabbit is indeed a wild animal, a fact confirmed when she eats her baby. Their concern then is to protect little Francis from the truth of a real 'rabbit' as opposed to a fantasy 'bunny'. Unfortunately, in trying to protect little Francis, his parents are to learn the equally disconcerting truth about their son. Just as they have hidden the reality of the rabbit behind the term 'little' pet, so too their son has been reduced by being seen as 'little' Francis. In both cases, Francis and Martha seem to yearn for the sense of something 'little', something vulnerable, to be cared for.

Both are given material comforts – little Francis is always well-dressed, his hair neatly combed – but little attention is paid to them emotionally. Both seem indifferent to the material care imposed on them. The rabbit 'never responded' to them, while little Francis displays a 'watchfulness' that is directed at them not the rabbit. Nor is the rabbit any 'more responsive to their humour than their son'. Little Francis seems more adult than the parents: he understands more about the nature of the rabbit, and doesn't resent the death of the baby, which amounts to a rejection of his parents.

In a sense, little Francis has been 'eaten' by his parents too, who have brought him up to conform to their own view of a child. They provide for him, but allow him no freedom to experience life at first hand. To Martha, however, his knowledge and acceptance of the rabbit makes clear that he, like the rabbit, is something monstrous, not the 'little pet' she had cherished. Through the small incident of bringing home the rabbit, a whole relationship is laid bare; the inadequacy of the parents is revealed in the inadequacy of their response to the rabbit and little Francis. It is little wonder that they are left shocked by the reality they discover about the rabbit and their son.

Consider the following:

1 Briefly list other phrases or exchanges that make clear the nature of the relationship between Francis and Martha and their son.

2 Do you think that Francis and Martha are good parents? Base your reasons on incidents from the story.

3 What is your impression of little Francis? What do you think he is like in school?

4 What differences would emerge had 'The Little Pet' been written in the first person, from little Francis's point of view? Consider actual incidents from the story.

5 Do you understand what little Francis means at the end of the story: '"Come here," he said to the rabbit. "I'm not cross with you. I knew you didn't like your baby."' Explain this fully.

Parents who try their best

In 'The Red Ball', rather than family tensions developing, we enter the story in the midst of tension, initially that of the son, Bolan. The family's moving has created the problem, and the story widens its focus to show how the whole family is under pressure. Through the issue of the red ball, they begin to come to terms with their predicament, with a sense of greater mutual understanding.

We are introduced to the isolation of Bolan, created by his family's moving away from the sugar cane fields of Tunapuna to the urban setting of Port of Spain, on the island of Trinidad. He feels disorientated, unable to accept the invitation to join an informal game of cricket. When he eventually joins in, his natural ability makes him quickly accepted. He remains wary, but returns home more settled. When he goes home, however, we see that the pressures are not on him alone.

His father resents both his being late home, and the opportunities that will come to Bolan through an education that was denied to him. His mother is more aware of the advantages that education might bring, which puts her into conflict with her husband. This conflict raises issues that reveal something of the past pressures on the husband-wife relationship, for example of money, and possibly of Bolan's intrusion. His father's demands on Bolan, his repeated use of the term 'boy', infuriate his mother but we can see his father's exhaustion – both through the day's work, and through the struggle their life has become, which is reflected in their meagre savings.

When, next evening, Bolan returns to the square to seek out his new friends, they have waited for his arrival. This fills him 'with an excitement he had never felt before'; he is 'pleased beyond words'. He has started to belong. However he comes too with a brand new 'red ball' and a determination to treat every-

Parents and Children

one after the game. His father's angry reappearance and accusations of thieving make it clear how Bolan has acquired the money. His mother tries to prevent the thrashing Bolan is given, sympathetically understanding that the ball he has bought with the money has become a mark of his acceptance within his new world. We learn that she has been aware of his initial difficulties in joining the cricket game. The conclusion of the story shows us a different perspective of the father, who in struggling to find a better life for them all, and particularly Bolan, has become too immersed in his own struggle and fatigue to appreciate the problems of adjustment faced by Bolan. Ironically, it is to safeguard Bolan's future that they have moved: '"is for you that we doin' all this . . . We love you like nothin' else in the whole, whole world"' but after the drama and expense of the move, it is too easy to lose sight of the object. They must all adjust.

Consider the following:

1 What is the significance of the red ball? Do you think this is the best title for the story? Give your reasons.
2 Do you think that the story would have been more successful if told in the first person, from Bolan's point of view? Give your reasons.
3 For which of the three characters do you feel most sympathy and why?
4 Is this a story that helps you to understand better the pressures that occasionally afflict your own family or that of friends? Why? Write about this in about 300–400 words.
5 Read 'The Living'[8]. What is it that makes the boy who tells the story aware of his family in a different way?
6 Choose any story you have read which you feel compares with 'The Red Ball' and write about its main incidents.

A child's need for independence

The mother in Doris Lessing's 'Through the Tunnel'[8] is outwardly cool, inwardly anxious, concerned for her son in a different way. We see the story from the outside, told in the third person by a narrator who shows us clearly the concerns of both mother and son. Again the title directs us to the central incident that demonstrates the tensions beneath the surface of the relationship.

The mother, a widow, worries 'conscientiously' over her relationship with her eleven-year-old son. She understands the danger of making him too dependent, but is also concerned for his well-being. Jerry, her son, is growing up and is looking to extend his boundaries. He is also anxious not to hurt his mother, responding to her with 'that unfailing impulse of contrition'.

They are on holiday, and the tension they are both aware of becomes apparent in the opening sentence of the story. The challenge and excitement of potential danger and the unknown are represented by 'a wild and rocky bay' while 'the crowded beach he knew so well from other years' represents the childhood security of things safe and known. Jerry, on the edge of adolescence, is between the two but the temptation of danger is becoming irresistible.

His mother's decision to allow him to go to the wilder bay brings neither of them any comfort. She goes worrying to the safe beach, while he, needing to look back for his mother, although 'relieved' that she is there, nevertheless feels 'all at once very lonely'. 'A foreigner', he is further isolated by meeting the local boys, whose language he does not speak, and with whose diving feats he cannot compete. He is reduced to acting the fool, the child coming out in him, to attract their attention.

Initially frightened by their diving skills, he resolves to try the feat himself: he wants to be accepted by the group of older boys. It becomes a kind of self-imposed initiation test to prove to himself his growing maturity and self-dependence. It was 'as if everything, the whole of his life, all that he would become, depended upon it ...' His determination and commitment, 'a most unchildlike persistence', drive him beyond his usual concern for his mother's wishes. His mother's beach now 'seemed a place for small children ... It was not his beach' as he continues his painstaking effort to improve his ability to stay under water.

The claustrophobic effect of his attempt on the tunnel is evoked closely – his eventual survival fortunate. His mother re-enters the narrative at the end, ironically, to point out the real distance between the two of them. She is concerned at his appearance, worried but reassures herself: '"Oh, don't fuss!

Parents and Children

Nothing can happen. He can swim like a fish."' Having achieved his very adult end, Jerry reverts to a child: '"Mummy ... I can stay under water for two minutes – three minutes at least"', which allows her to reassert her position. But the balance of the relationship has changed irrevocably.

Consider the following:

1 Briefly list the stages at which Jerry becomes determined to swim through the tunnel. Is the story convincing?
2 How does the author convey the tension and danger of the swim?
3 What kind of relationship do Jerry and his mother seem to have at the beginning of the story? (Look at the small details that suggest their feelings.) How has that relationship changed by the end?
4 Do you think Jerry's mother is a good mother? Give your reasons from evidence in the story.
5 What difference would there be had the story been told in the first person from Jerry's point of view?
6 Could a similar relationship exist between a daughter and mother? Would the 'test' of swimming through the tunnel be as appropriate to a girl? If not, what other test of independence would seem more appropriate?

The importance of the opening sentence

Parents who confuse their children

In the stories so far the title has directed us to the significant issue that reveals the reality of the relationships explored. The parents in these stories have tried to do their best for their children. In some cases though, tension and misunderstanding can arise from a situation in which families are left – perhaps through divorce or death. In John Wain's 'A Message from the Pig-Man'[8], and V.S. Naipaul's 'The Enemy'[4] such problems occur; in both stories, the opening sentence plunges us to the heart of the matter. Thereafter, the structure of each story is different, the former revolving around a single major incident, the latter conducted around a series of skirmishes that evolve into a resolution.

The opening sentence of 'A Message from the Pig-Man' makes clear the focus of the story. 'He was never called Ekky now, because he was getting to be a real boy, nearly six ... and his name was Eric ...' The story is seen through Eric's eyes, during the process of his 'growing up' and immediately that process is qualified by the uncritical way in which the opening words are presented. We may feel that six is rather young to be considered 'a real boy', and that he is merely reflecting what he has been told. Indeed we quickly learn that his mother and father have just separated, and that he is adjusting to 'Donald' moving in, although his mother has promised that '"nothing will be changed"'. When we see how he tries to make sense of the changes, we realize that he is too young to understand them. The suggestion that he is a 'real boy' seems to be rather the idea of the adults in the story, who hope it might help him to cope.

Eric's attempts to behave like a 'real boy' are tested over the issue of the Pig-Man. To a child, the notion of a Pig-Man suggests the qualities of both pig and man, a frightening notion. Eric has puzzled over the nature of this 'beast', confused that he is entrusted by normally protective parents to take out scraps – apparently to feed it. His inability to fathom out the nature of the beast is bracketed with his failure to come to terms with the disappearance of his father, culminating in the nightmare where both go off in a train together. Eric's desperate plea to his father, '"Don't bring the Pig-Man when you come back..."' reflects both his need for his father and his fear of the Pig-Man – both unresolved enigmas.

The 'crisis' arrives when his mother – in effect – forces him to confront the Pig-Man one evening. With considerable courage, Eric does so, and discovers the apparently simple truth that he is called the Pig-Man because '... he had some pigs that he looked after ...'. Unfortunately – from Eric's point of view – he feels that he has learned something. Instead of worrying about a problem, you merely face up to it and resolve it: 'You just went straight ahead ... You just did it.'

Life seems suddenly straightforward, particularly as there is another problem facing him, 'Why can't Dad be with us even if Donald is here?' The naïvety of the question is clear – to the adult world. His mother and Donald are pierced by his question, but fail to respond *to* him, instead talking *over* him. His mother treats him as if he were a small child, not the 'real' boy she has pretended he is. She refers to him as Ekky again, allows him to 'scrape out the basin'. He is understandably confused and infuriated by the change, which negates all he felt he had discovered. Now there is only anger: '... grown-ups were mad and silly and he hated them all, all, *all*.'

Consider the following:

1 How successfully do you think the author has presented the thoughts of a six-year-old in this story?

2 Do you think the Pig-Man was a necessary part of the story? Give your reasons.

3 Tell the story as if it was written in the first person from Eric's point of view.

4 Do you feel any sympathy for Eric? Refer to the story in some detail in your answer.

5 How well do you think the adults coped with Eric given the difficulties of the separation?

6 Do you understand Eric's final thoughts, that: '... grown-ups were mad and silly and he hated them all, all *all*'? Do you agree with his views here after what has happened?

A child's misunderstanding

The conflict within 'The Enemy' is made equally clear in the opening sentence: 'I had always considered this woman, my mother, as the enemy.' The structure of the story is less straightforward; a major instance – the circumstance of the boy's father's death – is followed by brief snapshots of his subsequent life with his mother. Their life together seems characterized by a strange bond of attraction and hatred, and it is only with the final incident, where he is buried by a falling wall, that we see what he felt the lack of – concern for him. The conclusion seems likely to bring a relationship based on mutual understanding in the future.

The nature of the story would be gloomy were it not for the way the story is told. The boy's tone shows little emotion and is at times flatly self-interested, creating a comic effect; after his parents separate, he stays with his father when he is promised a box of crayons. At his father's death he is more concerned that he will have to bear the burden of a father who was said to have died from fright: '... But in a month or so I had forgotten my father.' He throws casually into the narrative 'the day after Hat had rescued me from drowning at Docksite ...', and his final act, which nearly kills him, he describes as an imitation Superman act as he dives in front of the falling wall to prevent its fall.

The boy has little understanding of what his mother must have endured in the tension of living with his father, their arguments, her failure to have much influence over her son, which leads to his wounding decision to stay with his father rather than with her. Thereafter, her attempt to bring up her headstrong son is a testing experience which he seems to resist. Her determination to make him tie his shoelaces, to peel an orange, her resentment that there are other more useful or more intelligent boys, seem merely part of her need to have some claim over the child who is too easily identified with her unloved husband. '"You is your father child, you hear, not mine ..."' The boy is incapable of associating these continuing indications of care with the concern and anxiety he wants to see.

Genuine emotion comes only at the end as he comes round after the wall has crashed on top of him. Intact but for a broken hand, he sees his mother's eyes 'glassy and wet with tears'; what he has doubted throughout the story – that she was capable of being concerned and worried for him – becomes self-evident. The final paragraph, with its contradictory hope that he wished to enjoy once more his mother's tears, brings warmth into a story that has been one of conflict, though narrated in a wryly humorous way.

Consider the following:

1 Why does the boy prefer to stay with his father?
2 Does the mother actually hate her husband? How does this affect her relationship with the boy?

3 Make a list of the boy's good qualities, and another of his bad qualities. Would he make a good friend?

4 Was the boy's attitude to his mother fair?

5 In what ways is this an amusing story?

Assignments

1 Write diary entries of little Francis on the following occasions: on acquiring the rabbit; detailing his parents' attitude to the rabbit; on the parents' discovery that the rabbit has eaten its baby.
Suggested notes for your answer:

Initially: character of little Francis – taciturn – unenthusiastic – inward-looking – intelligent – cold – aware of parents' faults – personality important in expression of ideas.

First entry: little surprise at another attempt to please him – wonders when they will consult him over presents – irritation with their laughter, their excitement – show of token interest – decides to examine rabbit more closely when time on his own – resentment at being expected to be excited.

Second entry: as usual parents seem desperately too keen – why does father have to moan whenever he brings hutch in? – why does mother comment on price of lettuce? – they invent inappropriate names for rabbit – don't seem to know how many babies rabbits have – never actually handle rabbit – seem almost scared of her – on learning of baby rabbit's fate, disgust – never really try to understand it, or him . . .
Third entry: typically, they were surprised to discover rabbits eat runt of litter – knew they'd be disgusted, try to get rid of her – only way to stop them: to tell them I knew – Dad acted like child as usual, kicking hutch – Mum near hysterical then angry – thinks I've let her down – they just don't understand, rabbits or me.

2 By comparing 'The Enemy' with 'The Little Pet' or 'Message from the Pig-Man', try to explain why the authors used either the first or third person viewpoint to tell the story.

3 Imagine you were Bolan explaining to your mother why you

stole the money. What reasons would you give?

4 Write a letter from Bolan's mother to her sister in Tunapuna suggesting whether – in view of all that has happened – she regards the move as a success.

5 Write a letter from a grown-up Eric to his mother, resentful of the way she handled the separation, and the question of the Pig-Man.

6 Do you think that the boy's attitude to his mother in 'The Enemy' was fair? Compare his relationship with that of Jerry in 'Through The Tunnel'.

7 Imagine that the mothers of 'The Enemy' and 'The Red Ball' are old friends. Write a letter from the mother of 'The Enemy' to the other, explaining why she feels as she does about her son, and the way in which she has tried to bring him up.

8 Take any three of the stories considered here, and compare the attitudes of the parents to the children. With which do you feel most/least sympathy? How else do you feel they might have behaved towards their children?

9 Develop a general discussion on the relationship between parents and children – based on the details of your reading – using either the stories considered here or others that you have read. (For instance, 'My Oedipus Complex'[6], 'The Living'[8], 'The Key of the Cabinet'[5].) You should make detailed reference to at least *three* stories.

10 Why do you feel that all these stories concern relationships between boys and their parents? Read 'Growing up'[2] and 'The First Seven Years'[8]: are there differences between the way parents deal with daughters and sons?

11 For which of the boys here do you feel most sympathy? Why? (Compare them with those from other stories if you wish.) Consider at least *three* stories.

12 Compare the endings of any three of these stories (or others you have read on the same subject). Do they help to clarify the point of the story?

13 Write your own story of a relationship between parents and a child. (Will you write from first person or third person viewpoint? Will there be a key moment or a series of incidents? How important is the setting? How will it end – a twist? Will the title or first sentence point us to the nature of the conflict?)

A Significant Experience

In our youth, we are perhaps most vulnerable to a moment that may change the way our life develops – perhaps an accident, a death, or less dramatically a moment about which we have expectations, or which excites us. Our response to that moment may shape the way we think and develop in the future. Sometimes, of course, the way in which a young person responds may demonstrate that he or she is not yet ready to learn from the experience. The stories considered in this section are concerned with what are potentially significant moments for those faced with them.

Two stories might profitably be compared, Katherine Mansfield's story 'Her First Ball'[2] and Scott Fitzgerald's 'The Ice Palace'[2]. Both deal with young, inexperienced girls but do so in quite different ways. The titles help to point us towards the difference. 'Her First Ball' is meant literally: the story is concerned with Leila's excitement at attending her first ball. Fitzgerald's story is not about an ice palace, but about Sally-Carrol's desire to marry Harry Bellamy, and the ensuing differences between the Southern and Northern States of America that are revealed. The ice palace becomes a symbol – it represents all that Sally-Carrol eventually fears about the North: a wilderness, the cold, a sense of her being 'frozen, heart, body and soul.'

Turning points

Both girls are swept up by initial excitement, but Katherine Mansfield focuses entirely on the dance, while Fitzgerald presents Sally-Carrol's situation in a series of small incidents. Both stories are told in the third person, from the point of view of each girl, but there are differences here too. Leila's more naïve, inexperienced attitude is gently qualified by the author – for instance, Leila's enthusiasm makes her unable to see through the emptiness of her partners' conversation; Katherine Mansfield allows the reader to hear it. 'The Ice Palace' is told in a more neutral way, but we are most sympathetic towards Sally-Carrol, as it is through her eyes that we see the story develop. She is more mature too, and is able to glimpse possible problems with Harry, and after the experience of the ice palace, to understand that her real needs will not be met in the North with Harry.

In each story there is a 'significant moment' which tests the feelings of each girl. Leila's excitement and uncritical enthusiasm is confronted with the fat man's insensitive vision of her future, coloured by his own experience. What was bored indifference in the younger partners has hardened into cynicism in him – trapped within the triviality of such balls for thirty years, he almost takes delight in what he sees as her eventual end. That she should grow old and unattractive, immune to the pleasures of the ball, presumably mirrors his own failure to progress beyond such a world. For a moment, she is caught. 'Was this first ball only the beginning of her last ball, after all?' She is hurt: '... deep inside her a little girl threw her pinafore over her head and sobbed. Why had he spoiled it all?' She is saved by her youth and innocence, her capacity to lose herself once more in the ball, untroubled by any truth there may be in the fat man's words.

Sally-Carrol faces the real test of her feelings when trapped in the ice palace. The moment has been carefully prepared for. The difference between the South, from which Sally-Carrol has come, and Harry Bellamy's North has been partly depicted in terms of the climate, a climate that reflects the personalities of the inhabitants. Just as the South is warm, lazy, lethargic, and nostalgic for its past, so the North is cold, energetic, business-like and lives for the present. A typical inhabitant of the South seems 'feline' to Sally-Carrol, sensitive, open, while those from the North seem more 'canine', harder, more direct, less subtle. Sally-Carrol's visit to the ice palace brings to a head all the forebodings she has gradually felt about a future in the North. The ice palace can only be built at the coldest time of the year; trapped inside it after Harry's typically impulsive rush away, she feels herself 'alone with this presence that came out of the North ... an icy breath of death'. This seems to represent all she has met in the North, the rather cold, unfeeling welcome, the way her youthful enthusiasm has been humoured, Harry's insensitivity. She is rescued partly by what she feels is the presence of Margery Lee, for Sally-Carrol a symbol of the South, and is returned to the 'great warm nourishing bosom' of the South.

Both stories introduce us initially to the personality of the main character. Leila's excitement is presented through the way she feels that everything around her reflects the dance; the bolster in the cab felt 'like the sleeve of an unknown young man's suit', the scene outside the cab appears to her to be 'waltzing', and on her arrival at the ball she feels that the gas light 'was dancing already'. Our first impression of Sally-Carrol is of her laziness – even a yawn is too much effort. However, she is aware of the limitations of her life, of another side to her: 'there's a sort of energy – the feelin' that makes me do wild things.' We are brought close to the characters, even if we do not sympathize with them. While both face a telling moment in their lives, they react differently. Leila blocks out the possible truth of the fat man's words, while Sally-Carrol eventually makes a decision about her life, having already sensed – and tried to block out – the possibility that she was wrong about Harry and his North.

The short story identifies potential turning points in a character's life which may not always be apparent to us in real life. Like Leila, we may try to avoid a truth that may threaten our present enjoyment. Like Sally-Carrol, we may pursue a course of action that we feel to be right despite the warning of our deeper instincts.

Consider the following:

1 'Her First Ball' is told from Leila's point of view. Are we also made aware of the writer's point of view? Read the last paragraph of the story, for instance: how does Katherine Mansfield comment on Leila's actions?

2 How would each story differ were it told in the first person – with Leila or Sally-Carrol writing from the point of view of 'I'? Give details based on what happens in the story.

3 Write down the phrases that suggest the climate of the South in the first section of 'The Ice Palace', and that of the North in the third section. How does Fitzgerald suggest that the inhabitants share some of the qualities of the climate?

4 In what different ways is Leila's excitement made clear to us?

5 Compare the attitude of the dancing partners towards Leila (and say why they are presented through dialogue), with that of the young men at the dinner party who later dance with Sally-Carrol. Are there similarities between them? What kind

of conclusions do you think we are supposed to draw about them?

6 We could say that the shape of 'The Ice Palace' is circular: Sally-Carrol ends up where she started. The six sections deal with different aspects of the South or the North. There are perhaps parallels between sections I and III, and between II and IV. Try to work out what each section is mainly concerned with.

7 Would 'Her First Ball' be successful without the fat man's comments? 'Was it – could it all be true?' Are the fat man's comments 'true'? Do they matter or change anything?

8 What aspects of her first disco/dance might catch the attention of an excited girl today? How would they differ from the aspects that might strike a boy in the same situation?

Assignments

1 What differences emerge between South and North in 'The Ice Palace'? Do you feel that Fitzgerald has a preference?
Suggested notes for essay answer:

Introduction: 'There's two sides to me, you see' (p. 158) – story's opening section reveals both Sally-Carrol's energy and passivity – story makes clear how one side represented by North, one by South – ice palace seems to show inferiority of North – concern with past/dead conveys criticism too of South.

Paragraph 2: Section I opens with images of South – lethargic – passive – warm – happy – contrast with energy of Harry – 'tall, broad and brisk' – Sally-Carrol's enjoyment of graveyard – the Confederate dead.

Paragraph 3: Section III shows images of North – cold – isolation – listless – Harry's pride and energy – contrast of Sally-Carrol's enthusiasm.

Paragraph 4: Dinner-party draws distinction between canine and feline – begin to see nature of Northern people – 'gradually getting gloomy and melancholy' – Bellamy women – 'spiritless conventionality' – Harry's attitude to Southerners – 'hangdog, ill-dressed, slovenly lot'.

English coursework: The Short Story

Paragraph 5: Climax of Sally-Carrol lost in ice palace – symbolic of being lost in wastes of the North – return.

Conclusion: Some distinctions are those of climate – affects too the people – Southerners warmer – sensitive – Northerners seem cold – but too, Southern tendency to dwell on past – look back not forward – slow – passive – contrast of North's ability to look to future – to achieve – Fitzgerald perhaps sees strengths and weaknesses in both South and North – because we identify with Sally-Carrol, perhaps a sense that the South seems a more sympathetic place.

2 Write some extracts from Sally-Carrol's diary of her impressions of the Northern states and the people she meets (from section III onwards), *or* After Sally-Carrol's return to Tarleton, write a letter from Harry to a friend outlining his feelings about Southerners.

3 Imagine that Leila stays on with the Sheridans after the ball. Write the letter she might write to her mother with her impressions of the ball.

4 With whom do you identify more, Leila or Sally-Carrol? Why?

5 Which of the two stories do you find more satisfying? Why?

6 Mr Quick faces a significant moment in 'Growing Up'[2] as do the boy and Mickser in 'The Living'[8]. What do they learn from their experiences?

7 Have you read other stories where characters have faced a significant moment, a turning point perhaps, in their lives? Compare their experiences with those here – consider at least *three* stories.

Turning points – the consequences

The moments in which two younger characters become involved in adult activities are in one case tragic, and in the other potentially damaging. In Jan Carew's 'Hunters and Hunted'[4], Tonic's desire to join his father and brothers on a hunting trip leads to a horrifying accident, while in Hemingway's 'Indian Camp'[2], it is the decision of Nick's father to take Nick with him on a medical visit to a squalid Indian camp that leads to the unexpected and gruesome climax. Neither boy understands what he has become involved in, but while Tonic's inexperience and excitement contribute to the tragedy, Nick's youth protects him from the significance of what he sees.

Like the previous two stories, 'Indian Camp' is told in the third person, but through the eyes of the central character, Nick. 'Hunters and Hunted' is told from the outside, like a report of what happened, and though we are closer to Tonic's view of the action, it is his brother, Tengar, who registers what happens. In both stories we are looking at a single incident in a family relationship, and while we are drawn to the story itself, our interest may also be drawn to what it suggests about the relationships.

The stories may also arouse our curiosity about what is not shown of the characters, in a way that the previous stories fail to do. For instance, while 'Hunters and Hunted' shows a hunting trip, even before the story reaches its climax we are made aware of the tensions between the father and brothers. Each born of different mothers, the brothers are very different. Tonic is bright, and is being encouraged to study, which causes some resentment, certainly with Caya. Tengar is protective towards Tonic, even to the extent of crossing his father. Doorne is struggling to maintain his authority among strong older sons, and feels that Tonic should be educated, but also that he should learn traditional ways; proud of his education, he is exasperated by his complaints of the difficulty of the trip. Ironically, it is Tonic's death that pulls them together again.

We are aware too in 'Indian Camp' that it is odd for a father to take his son to see a caesarian operation. The few glimpses we gain of the father, the comments of Uncle George about him, give us only a fleeting impression but one which might intrigue us about the relationship, about the 'unwritten' story of their lives, of which this is only a tiny instance.

The 'significant moment' of 'Indian Camp' is when Nick's father turns his attention to the father of the child he has just delivered. The discovery of the man's cut throat accentuates to a great extent what we have learned of the father. He is shocked at what his son has been forced to witness, although he has not thought of the consequences of allowing his son to witness a bloody and disturbing operation. The impression of Nick's father that we have received is of his precise and clinical manner: 'This lady is going to have a baby' and the subsequent detail of what will happen. In the course of the delivery, when the mother is screaming, he says: '"But her screams are not important. I don't hear them because they are not important."' However, he also seems to take great pride in what he has achieved: '"That's one for the medical journal, George."'

What he has not allowed for is the possible effect on Nick, whether it is appropriate, for instance, for a young child to act as 'interne' to such a disturbing experience – quite apart from the suicide of the Indian. It seems to be part of Nick's relationship with his father that he is assumed to 'know' what his father is talking about ('I know', 'I see'), although he clearly understands less than he suggests. Faced with the reality of the operation, he soon loses this assumed indifference. Understandably upset by the woman's screaming, he is unable to observe the operation. 'Nick did not watch. His curiosity had been gone for a long time.' What is more remarkable is that eventually, rowing home, we learn that little of the incident has touched him: 'in the stern of the boat with his father rowing, he felt quite sure that he would never die.' His youth, his innocence, protect him in the end.

Perhaps the father has learned more than the child. Screams *are* important. Trapped by his wounded foot, unable to escape the sound of his wife's screams, the Indian father faces perhaps the final element in a life that may already have brought him to the edge of despair. (Consider the squalid nature of the camp – the level to which the once proud possessors of the land have been reduced, anything noble or romantic in their past has disappeared.) Perhaps Nick's father needs to be reminded of the human significance of what he does. He seems unaware of the significance of Uncle George's comment and absence.

Tonic's fate is tragic. He pays for his innocence and inexperience. The whole trip to the Black Bush has been quite different from his expectations. It is more exhausting than he realized or expected. His father and brothers have not expected his response. They react in different ways; Doorne is proud of his son's intelligence, but concerned too that he understands what has been his family's way of life. While he has encouraged his study, he is not certain that it will help him. 'Even if he is bright like moonlight on still water, it is time he understand he can't live by book alone.' Caya seems resentful, teasing Tonic and his father's expectations of him, and after Tonic's death, more preoccupied with the price the hogs would bring in the village than with his brother's death. Tengar is more affectionate, protective towards Tonic, more aware of the difficulties of the trip.

The crucial moment of the story – when Tonic fires Tengar's gun and finds himself thrown into the middle of the hogs – has been well prepared. Tonic's dream of wolves and the man whose 'mouth was always dripping blood' already suggests his eventual end. We see it too in the fate of the jaguar submerged beneath the pack, however powerfully he has fought. Once Tonic sees the possibility of firing the shotgun, whilst the others are lost in the jaguar's struggle, the tragedy is liable to happen. The ferocity of the hogs' attack is horrifying, Tonic's death appalling. For a moment it brings together again the rest of the family, but Tengar's final comment echoes that of many people faced with death – why? What did Tonic die *for*?

In both stories then, we are faced with a significant moment in the lives of the main characters, a moment though that also suggests a wider sense of their family – both fathers have an important role in the crisis each son faces. The interest of each story lies partly in what is *not* told. Both raise questions about the nature of death. The fact of death is perhaps the most challenging question of living, whether in making sense of it, which Tengar finds understandably difficult, or in confronting it when you are too young to make sense of it, as Nick does. In many other stories we meet, the central incident revolves around death, and how the main characters respond to it, whether they can, or how they do, cope with the consequences.

Consider the following:

1 Do you think that Nick gained anything from his visit to the Indian camp? Give your reasons.

2 Would we have learned more about Nick's reaction had the story been told in the first person? Would anything in the story have been lost by this manner of telling?

3 What differences would there have been if Tengar had told the story of 'Hunters and Hunted'?

4 In 'Indian Camp', Uncle George says of Nick's father, 'Oh,

you're a great man, all right', and then disappears. Why?

5 Compare the first paragraph of 'The Ice Palace' with the three short opening paragraphs of 'Indian Camp'. What differences do you find in the way the opening scenes are described? (Then turn to the section on 'Style'.)

6 Both these stories deal with uncomfortable, disturbing moments of pain or violence. Is there anything to be learned from such stories, or would we be better off without them?

7 Would the fathers in these two stories have anything to share after the experiences that their children suffer?

8 What other stories that you have read have been concerned with death in some way? How do they differ from these two?

9 The four stories considered in this section described young people faced with a particular moment in their life which has led to conflicting conclusions – from the death of one, to the capacity to shrug off the experience in two others. What other stories have you read that face a young person with such a crucial early experience? How do they compare with any of these?

10 Which of the four stories do you prefer? Explain why.

Assignments

1 Was anyone to blame for Tonic's death? Explain in some detail what you feel about this.
Suggested notes for essay answers:

Introduction: Apparent background to hunting trip – Tonic wants to hunt – part of the life of his family – father confused – admires Tonic's education – feels he must learn family skills too – Caya slightly resentful of Tonic's education – Tengar strong and indulgent older brother – all are aware of dangers – do not feel Tonic at particular risk.

Paragraph 2: After Tonic's initial exhaustion, enthusiasm – in the forest – lively – excited – fidgety – on platform, Tonic warned of danger of falling.

Paragraph 3: Temptation of loaded shotgun to excited boy – cannot resist opportunity – when he falls, Tengar fights heroically for him – little that Caya and Doorne can do.

Conclusion: In one sense, Tonic's own action caused his death – his excitement inevitable? – should others have watched him more closely? – Doorne to blame for bringing a young child on dangerous hunt? – Tengar to blame for not noticing Tonic take shotgun? – or just Fate? – Tengar's anger: 'But why Tonic die, tell me that?'

2 We only glimpse what Nick was like. Try to imagine a letter he might have written to a friend giving his impression of the visit to the Indian camp.

3 Compare the fathers in 'Indian Camp' and 'Hunters and Hunted'. Why do you think each was prepared to allow his son to face his particular experience? Do you feel sympathy for either?

4 Some stories are more ordinary than others. 'Indian Camp' and 'Hunters and Hunted' offer incidents out of the ordinary. Do you find them convincing – can you believe them? Can an 'ordinary' person learn anything from them?

5 Which style of writing do you prefer, Hemingway's or Fitzgerald's? What differences are there between the two? What different effects do you like or dislike in the way they write?

6 Compare two other stories that you have read which deal with death or other significant moments in the life of a young person with one or more of those discussed here. Consider similarities or differences – which has seemed to you the most striking? (You might, for instance, consider Sillitoe's 'On Saturday Afternoon'[7], Mary Lavin's 'The Living'[8] or Michael Anthony's 'Drunkard of the River'[4].)

7 Have you ever faced a moment that you feel might have changed your life? It will not necessarily be as dramatic as some faced here. Try to write a story about it (will you write as 'he' or 'she' or 'I'?) as a single moment, or a series of small incidents? Who else was involved – how much do we need to know of them? Will you concentrate on the moment itself or your reaction to it? Is it only important for what it meant to you, or does it suggest as much about others around you?

The Outsider

Many short stories deal with ordinary people having to adjust or respond to an incident that is out of the ordinary. Sometimes though it is the person who is out of the ordinary, and it is those around him or her who are affected or have to respond in some way. Such stories are more often about the individual's relationship with society, a society that often has fixed ideas as to how people should behave. It can be 'society' in a wider sense – all of us – or in the narrow sense of a group of people who perhaps share the same interest or, as in 'Late Night on Watling Street'[5], the same job. Again, it is often a particular moment that brings to a head the tensions or conflict between the individual and society. In the stories discussed here, it is difficult always to know where our sympathies lie – society sometimes reaches hasty judgements about people just as individuals feel let down by such judgements at times.

Victims

Both Ernest Brown in 'Uncle Ernest'[8] and John Elsen in 'The Road'[2] feel out of place in the worlds in which they find themselves. Ernest Brown has been broken by his experiences in the First World War, to which his thoughts constantly return. He feels guilt at his own survival where so many of his contemporaries were killed. Life has become for him a purposeless routine, in which he has neglected his own appearance, spending any spare money on beer which brings him temporary forgetfulness. He is isolated from society around him, feeling 'utterly unhappy and empty'.

After ten years at sea, six of which were spent in the Second World War, John Elsen's real home is his ship. He leaves to seek his family in his home town but is disoriented on land, in a town he no longer recognizes, which has clearly suffered damage during the war. Stepping into the street 'was like stepping into the maelstrom' (the maelstrom was a huge whirlpool found in the sea). His excitement at meeting his family again is checked by his confusion and failure to locate the street in which they live: 'he felt sad, lost, angry.'

Both stories are told in the third person, but we are perhaps closer to Elsen, whose thoughts are shared with us directly. We understand enough about Ernest's feelings and past to enable us to understand what his friendship with the girls means to him. Both stories develop gradually rather than relying on a significant moment; while both contain a moment when the story reaches its climax, that moment has come to seem inevitable in each. As readers, we may feel that we understand the developing situations more clearly than the characters themselves. The way in which they develop depends on those secondary to the main characters whose behaviour is a significant part of each story's effect.

Ernest's loneliness has been reduced by meeting the girls – his relationship with them has given his life a sense of purpose. Because the story is in the third person we can be told how he was 'wholly absorbed in doing good'; he feels a kind of paternal affection, seeing the girls 'almost as his daughters ... the only people he had to love'. We are told too though of his rather naïve 'oblivious contentment', and already know of his appearance, which he further neglects in looking after the girls. He is unaware of the impression he must make on others. His dream is brought to a brutal end by the insensitive treatment of the policemen, who misinterpret his motives. Their reference to 'men like you' sums up society's attitudes, which tends to judge people from the outside.

In the course of 'The Road', Elsen meets a succession of individuals from the barman to Mr Herron, all of whom show themselves prepared to be helpful to an extent but not really to become involved in his predicament. We learn that Elsen himself is not particularly talkative, and the people with whom he comes into contact tend to talk in short, broken sentences. His increasing confusion, anger and isolation stem partly from this rather fragmented world, in which there seems no order, nobody who can really help. Some of those he meets seem to want to help, but, as with the barman and conductor, do little more than get rid of Elsen, who is becoming something of a problem to them.

As readers, we may feel that we understand the situation more quickly than Elsen. While he is bewildered and lost, we may begin to suspect, as a result of the policeman's response, that something more serious is wrong. We may feel too that he has sensed something wrong throughout – with his family's failure to write, for instance, but he seems unwilling to face such a truth. The whole story is told in a rather stumbling awkward way (consider for instance pp. 82–3) to reflect Elsen's situation as it gradually becomes apparent. We feel his frustration as again and again he receives apparently helpful, friendly responses which fail to solve his central problem. Because we see it from Elsen's point of view, we feel obvious sympathy for him, but we too may understand the reaction of other characters, their reserve, perhaps fear, at becoming too involved.

We may feel sympathy for Mrs Gurney's response – she is quick to see that he has been away and does not know what has happened to the street. She is sympathetic, but cannot face telling Elsen what she suspects. She and Fred are well-meaning but send him on to Father Tumilty for the truth. Passed on once more, he is finally told the truth by Mr Herron in the climax to which the story has been building. There is no hesitation here, no attempt to soften the blow – the ex-warden becomes so full of pride at his own full records of the incident that he forgets the human cost entirely, forgetting even Elsen's name. Brutally, he reads out the names of his entire dead family, and while making a show of sorrow, is left contemplating his records and how useful they have been.

Both Elsen and Ernest are difficult to help, living within their own worlds almost outside the society in which they live. Elsen's ten-year absence has made the world he used to know quite alien to him. Ernest's guilt at surviving the war has made him isolate himself from the world. Society's response to them is different: there is a reluctance to become involved in Elsen's plight particularly the closer to the truth people get. Ernest is judged on his appearance – no attempt is made to understand his actions. Both men find communication difficult which leaves them open to the rather brutal climax of each story, one at the hands of the police, acting from the best motives, the other at the hands of an unsympathetic and unthinking man, who cares more for facts than for people.

Consider the following:

1 It is made clear by the way the story is told that Ernest is innocent of what the police suspect in 'Uncle Ernest'. List ways

in which we are made aware of his innocence. Had the story been written in the first person would his innocence have been as clear? Consider the list you have just made – would the same methods have been possible had the story been told by Ernest as himself?

2 Similarly, had 'The Road' been told in the first person, what effect would there be on the story – particularly the way in which other people speak to Elsen? (Try rewriting the conversation between Elsen and the policeman for instance, or the last page or so of the story with Elsen in the first person – discuss the difficulties and effects.)

3 What two sentences haunted Ernest? Why has he made no attempt to make contact with people he knew previously? What is wrong with him?

4 Why does he befriend the two girls? (Consider the way he defends himself against the accusations of the policemen – how does he see the relationship?)

5 Do you think that Elsen ever suspects the truth about his family? Suggest which moments in the story lead you to this conclusion. Do you think he should have realized the truth earlier? If so, when?

6 Look closely at each of the conversations Elsen has (with the barman, conductor, the lady on the bus, the policeman, second conductor, Mrs Gurney, Father Tumilty and Mr Herron). Are there similarities in the way they respond? (Consider the way they express themselves.) Do you feel that any of them really care for Elsen? Which of them do you dislike most?

7 What impression are you left with of Elsen?

Assignments

1 Write a report as if you were one of the policemen, giving details of your observation of Ernest, and the reasons for your actions.
Suggested notes for essay answer:

Paragraph 1: Alerted to problem of Ernest Brown, Upholsterer,

English coursework: The Short Story

by two market traders – regulars of Greasy Chip café – they'd become concerned about welfare of two young girls – girls had been visiting café over period of two months – always making for table of Brown – dishevelled appearance – dirty – smelly clothes – no collar to shirt – he bought them anything they wanted each day – older girl increasingly making demands – he constantly gave in to them.

Paragraph 2: Began observation of subject – continued over three days – Brown certainly in need of wash – gave impression of a down-and-out – seemed very fond of girls – spent a lot of money on them on food – older girl constantly asking for money – presents – he gave them more money – seemed something not quite right – followed subject after girls left – did not go with them but returned to shabby digs.

Paragraph 3: Nothing unpleasant seemed to have happened – yet – seemed to be buying their confidence though – felt we ought to warn him off before situation worsened – approached him in café – established that girls weren't relations – told him to leave them alone – predictably tried to make a fuss – took him out – up the street – warned him.

Paragraph 4: Don't feel any other action necessary – will check café later in week – talk to market traders – believe he got the message – seemed rather pathetic – frightened, dirty old man.

and

Write a short letter from Mr Herron to one of his fellow wardens who has since moved away, giving an account of Elsen's visit and your reaction to it.

2 Write a short account of what happens to either Elsen or Ernest in the future.

3 Compare the characters of Elsen and Ernest. Do you feel more sympathy for one or the other?

4 Compare the endings of the two stories. Were the police right to behave as they did? Was Mr Herron right to give Elsen the truth in such a direct way? What do we learn from the reaction of each character to what they hear?

5 Do you feel that there was any more sympathetic way of

dealing with the problems of Elsen or Ernest?

6 Both stories seem in some ways depressing. Can we learn anything from them? Do they change the way we may behave in any way?

7 Both stories are about men. Write an account of a lonely or isolated woman, and the ways in which people respond to her.

8 Compare either/both stories with others that deal with characters isolated in their own world, or who have been cut off from their past. (Consider perhaps 'The Secret Life of Walter Mitty'[2] – is this as depressing as the two above? or 'Cane is Bitter'[4] – does this seem more positive at the end?)

The key moment – reported

We all have to acknowledge the strength of social pressure. There are certain things – as Ernest Brown discovered – that are frowned upon. Such rules are often unwritten, but powerful for all that. In 'Late Night on Watling Street'[5], Jackson ignores many of the accepted practices that make the group of lorry drivers we meet so close-knit and supportive. Much time is spent in creating the atmosphere in the 'caff', and its underlying tensions, all of which focus on Jackson. The fact that he is always referred to by his surname emphasizes that he is outside the group. His relationship with Ethel, his hostility towards Willie, his attempt to humiliate Lew, the way he breaks the easy atmosphere of the 'caff', almost starting a fight, all count against him. Even then, though, the others are capable of showing sympathy to him on hearing of his latest speeding offence, as the 'matey feeling came up ... the feeling of all being drivers and the law always after you', particularly as the police officer responsible, 'Babyface', uses what they regard as underhand methods to catch speeding drivers.

The story is told in the first person, through the eyes of Bolton, an experienced and respected driver. He is a decent, straightforward man, whose judgement of Lew (for instance, 'I hate fakes and show offs and Lew's one') is fairly balanced by his acknowledgement that 'they say he's good for a touch if you're short of cash'. It is through Bolton that we understand the 'code' by which the drivers live, for instance the way they are united by their feelings towards the police. We can see too, however, some of the limitations of the first-person viewpoint and how they can be overcome. Bolton cannot 'see' the climax of the story, because it involves another character. Thus the 'significant moment' of the story happens 'off-stage'. However, the moment has been engineered carefully. In the discussion about the danger of police cars 'tailing a lorry', we are told: '"I saw Jackson suddenly take an interest."' When he asks Bolton for the loan of a driving mirror, he questions him carefully about police procedures, and we learn that the charge against him will be one of dangerous driving; there is also a suspicion that he tried to bribe 'Babyface'. He checks carefully how many police witnesses are needed to proceed with the case. His comments '"I could murder the perishing lot of 'em . . . I'd sooner cut their throats"' suggest the strength of his feelings. As he leaves with the mirror, we might suspect his intentions.

Although Bolton cannot 'see' the crash, he arrives quickly afterwards. We 'hear' what happens in Jackson's confession to Bolton, a confession marked by his lack of remorse, almost a sense of vicious satisfaction at what has been in effect, murder: '"Nothing I like better than getting one across the law."' Bolton does not know how to register what he is told, though we feel his uneasiness. The final paragraph of the story brings out the effect of what Jackson has done. Like the reader of the story, the drivers have understood what has happened: 'as for Jackson, not a word was spoken.' While their 'code' prevents their informing on Jackson to the police (an accusation that might be difficult to prove in any case), they will punish him by exclusion from their community, making clear their contempt for him. Ethel's identification with the drivers makes his punishment more telling.

Consider the following:

1 How would the story be different were it told from the outside like a report of the events?

2 What things has Jackson on his mind when he enters the 'caff'? Why was he speeding?

3 What do you think has brought Jackson and Ethel together? Is it to do with Lew and if so why does Ethel not go off with Jackson?

4 How do the other drivers view the relationship between Ethel and Jackson? What impression do we get of Lew's feelings for Jackson?

5 Why are the other drivers particularly aggressive towards Babyface? Briefly consider what impression we get of Babyface – particularly in terms of his nickname.

6 Looking in detail at Jackson's behaviour in the story, what impression do you gain of him?

7 Was Jackson's plan to trap Babyface in any way justified?

8 Was the drivers' response to Jackson at the end of the story the right one? Should Bolton have gone straight to the police? Why doesn't he?

Assignments

1 Write an account of how Jackson prepares his lorry, traps Babyface, and explains his actions to the police afterwards from a third-person viewpoint.

Suggested notes for essay answers:

Paragraph 1: Needs to deal first with Babyface's habit of creeping up behind lorry obscured by lorry's load – borrows driving mirror from Jackson – takes up floorboard from cab of lorry – positions mirror underneath cab – gives view behind lorry of Babyface approaching – gets hold of old overcoat – stows it in lorry.

Paragraph 2: Waits for sight of Babyface – sees him without lights behind him – speeds up down Long Hill – knows place where Babyface will overtake – just before they reach it, brakes hard – police car too close to avoid collision – smashes into back of lorry – Jackson pulls up – removes mirror – replaces floorboard – places coat under lorry.

Paragraph 3: Convinces police that coat was mistaken for person – explains braking – suggests that police car had no lights – pretends shock – gets rid of mirror.

and

English coursework: The Short Story

Write a detailed account of the scene when Babyface stops Jackson, from a third-person viewpoint (considering what we know of Jackson, his reason for speeding, what the other drivers suggest about Babyface, the charge of dangerous driving, and the possible 'bribe').

2 Write an account from Bolton's point of view, of a conversation he has with Ethel some time after the events described. (What is Bolton's attitude to Jackson now? How does Ethel feel – regrets, lingering sympathy, anger . . .?)

3 Considering his feelings for Ethel as well as the behaviour described in the story, what do you feel about Jackson?

4 Imagine the story stopped when Jackson borrowed the driving mirror from Bolton . . . how else might the story finish? (Use any clues the story might have suggested.) *or* By looking closely at what Bolton says, explain why we might have expected the story to end as it did . . . including any details that you do not think were followed up, and any details that might have suggested a different ending.

5 Was Jackson's punishment a just one? Should Bolton have told the police the truth?

6 Compare this story with any other you have read where the central character(s) break the code of his or her (or their) society. Which do you find the more convincing? Give reasons for your answer.

The importance of the setting

A more complex story than any of these, Graham Greene's 'The Destructors'[7], considers T or Trevor, an 'outsider' within the Wormsley Common Gang. Many details suggest ways in which he is different: his name, his father's former occupation as an architect, his brooding silence: 'There was every reason why T . . . should have been an object of mockery.' Nor does it help when he tells them that Old Misery's house was built by Sir Christopher Wren, and that the staircase and panelling are two hundred years old. He describes the house as 'beautiful' – Blackie is on the verge of ridiculing T: 'It was the word 'beautiful' that worried him – that belonged to a class world . . . He was tempted to say "My dear Trevor, old chap"...' T saves himself only by his suggestion that they destroy the house.

The setting of the story is important. Immediate post-war London was scarred by bomb damage – Old Misery's house is a clear example – but also by economic depression and unemployment. Socially too, the war had changed the nature of class structure throwing together those formerly quite distinct from one another. Children too had suffered, and we see in the gang the results of childhood deprivation; this is a generation whose development has been distorted by the war. Normal creative feelings struggle to find expression – so that T, who has both an appreciation of beauty and a creative desire, perhaps inherited from his father, can only direct it to a negative, destructive end. T's experiences have undermined him; he is deeply disturbed (he has 'eyes as grey and disturbed as the drab August day').

Much that is positive goes into the destruction, as Blackie notices: 'He had at once the impression of organization, very different from the old happy-go-lucky ways'; they are described as working 'with the seriousness of creators – and destruction after all is a kind of creation'. The kind of social system that had led to Wren's creative ability seems to have collapsed in the post-war situation; his inheritors are able only to destroy, but with the same energy and creativity that he brought to architecture. Wren's house becomes a symbol of the old order, like the image of the top hat; for a moment the house 'had stood there with such dignity between the bombsites like a man in a top hat'. The new values are represented by the lorry driver who laughs at the end, quite unable to appreciate Old Misery's feelings.

T may seem outside the gang initially, but they are united in having been emotionally maimed by their experiences of the war. Theirs is a generation that has no contact with pre-war society or values, a prospect that clearly worries Graham Greene. They are all outside the society that he seems to value. They seem to value nothing: 'All this hate and love ... it's soft, it's hooey. There's only things ...'

Consider the following:

1 How convincing do you find the story? While reading the story is it easy to accept that destroying such a house is possible? Why?

English coursework: The Short Story

2 Compare T and Blackie – whose gang would you rather be in?

3 What do you consider the 'significant moment' of the story?

4 Why does the lorry driver laugh at the end? What does it suggest about him? Would you have laughed?

5 Do you feel sympathy for Old Misery?

Assignments

1 What impression do you get of the adult world from the story? (Consider Blackie's desire to impress the older gangs (p. 174), the reaction of the parents to some of the children in the gang, Old Misery, the lorry driver.) Do you think the way the adults behave has had any influence on the children in this story?

Suggested notes for essay answer:

Introduction: Post-war world with different values – new emerging culture represented by gangs – illicit betting – violent and callous.

Paragraph 2: Old Misery – survivor of old culture – Wren-built house – tries to be sympathetic – chocolates – but looks too for sense of order (p. 183 'Only it's got to be regular') – no place for order in anarchy of gang system – Blackie interested in T's idea because it might impress 'even the grown-up gangs'.

Paragraph 3: Mike's parents – threats against his straying – but sent to Church alone – they have overdone Saturday night – little genuine moral guidance – Summers given 'a bob for slot machines' – next stage the 'betting at the all-in wrestling'.

Paragraph 4: Response of lorry driver is callous – representative of a generation immune to the human reality of violence/loss – hardened by suffering of war – can only laugh.

Conclusion: Old Misery stands alone as part of social system now in decay – other adults show hypocrisy – materialism – part of gangs or criminality – callous – insensitive – values which appear to have influenced the Wormsley Common car-park gang – particularly T.

2 Write an account of a conversation Blackie has with a friend some years later in which he recalls T, and the incident described in the story. (Include his impressions of T, and the reason why he helped him when Old Misery returned unexpectedly.) Write it in the form of a letter if you prefer.

3 Why do you think T wanted to destroy the house?

4 Write a letter from Old Misery to a friend in which he describes the events of the Bank Holiday Monday.

5 Do you find the story in any way amusing – as the lorry driver seems to?

6 Compare T with Soni in 'Drunkard of the River'[4]. Whose behaviour do you find more disturbing?

7 Write your own story of a child disturbed by living in the present. (What aspect of modern life might have made him disturbed? How might he express his feelings – can you imagine an incident comparable to destroying a house? How do the adults in his life behave?)

8 Compare any of the four stories in this section with others you have read which deal with 'outsiders' (there are some suggestions earlier in the section). How do they differ from these stories? Which do you prefer?

Living with the consequences

So far we have considered mainly stories that present us with a key moment which brings to a head the tensions or conflict facing the characters. Other stories may present us with the moments that follow the crucial incident, and the centre of interest in the story becomes the way in which the characters deal with the consequences of what has happened. Such stories, like 'Daughters of the Late Colonel'[1], do not necessarily offer any further key incidents, but instead concentrate on showing how the characters continue to live in the shadow of what has happened. Others, like 'Samphire'[2], while showing the continuing life of the characters, still depend on a further incident to bring out the real tension.

All the stories considered in this section are related in some way to death. 'Daughters of the Late Colonel' and 'Samphire' chart meticulously the relationships between, respectively, two sisters, and a married couple. Both relationships are almost unbearably claustrophobic, and while the sisters remain too repressed by the memory of their father to change their lives, Molly is moved to attempt murder by the circumstances of her marriage.

Moments in a life

A repressive father

Our initial impression of Constantia and Josephine in 'Daughters of the Late Colonel'[1] might be that they are like children – their conversation is odd, unrealistic, but it becomes increasingly clear that while they might appear childish, they are not children. Their present condition has everything to do with their father and his treatment of them, as the story makes clear. The ferocity of Colonel Pinner is suggested in many ways: the 'dark, angry purple' of his face, Mr Farolles' panic at almost sitting in the Colonel's chair, his short explosive interview with Cyril, but most obviously through the reaction of the sisters.

The structure of the story underlines the dreariness of the sisters' lives in which little has ever happened; time is measured in terms of a change of servants. Thus there is no narrative, no 'story' element here; instead we are presented with several sections each representing a small episode that reflects their lives and attitudes. Fear of their father is common to each; even with his death, they are dominated by the sense that he is still there. Jug fears 'that father was in the chest of drawers', and even the funeral cannot reassure them: 'What would father say when he found out... Buried. You two girls had me buried!'

With so little to occupy them, they compensate by becoming embarrassingly preoccupied with small details which seem painfully trivial to others. Thus Josephine can become almost sharp when Cyril cannot recall whether his father is 'still so fond of meringues', a memory that becomes unbearably central to Cyril's subsequent conversation with Colonel Pinner. Neither sister has much grasp of reality, as we see from section X; Jug struggles harder to face practical decisions, while Con drifts constantly into vague daydreams. They have never been given the confidence to advance beyond their present childlike state.

Colonel Pinner's death, however, does open up the possibility of life invading their existence once more. The richness of the description of the organ grinder's notes, 'a perfect fountain of bubbling notes shaking from the barrel-organ, round, bright notes, carelessly scattered' awakens a sense of 'something' that Con cannot quite recall, 'almost a pain and yet a pleasant pain'. Josephine too remembers: 'another life... But it all seemed to have happened in a kind of tunnel. It wasn't real.' Their memories are accompanied – symbolically – by the richness of the colour of the sunshine that 'thieved' its way in: red, almost golden.

The story's conclusion appears to reject the 'happy ending' that might perhaps seem untruthful in the circumstances. Just as the sisters begin to glimpse what might be within their grasp – a future that might fulfil some of their dreams – they return to the state in which for too long they have remained. On the verge of a significant statement, their conversation collapses at the very end of the story, Con forgetting 'what it was... that I was going to say'. Symbolically again, a cloud covers the sun as Josephine replies: '"I've forgotten too."'

Consider the following:

1 Like most of Katherine Mansfield's short stories, this is most minutely and delicately observed. Nothing 'exciting' happens and yet we learn much about the characters. Why, at first, might we think Con and Jug are children? When do we first suspect that they are not?

2 List all the details that give some impression of Colonel Pinner. What sort of man does he seem to be?

3 Why is the story divided into different sections? Do any seem similar or are they all different? Is there a 'significant moment' to the story? If so, where? If not, why not?

4 Through whose eyes do we see the story, Con's, Jug's or both? What differences emerge between them?

5 What do we learn of Con and Jug through their reactions to Nurse Andrews, and to Kate?

6 What impression does Cyril make? Do you feel any sympathy for him?

7 Briefly list the reactions of Con and/or Jug to their father's death. How do their reactions suggest their father's influence upon them?

8 What is your eventual impression of Con and Jug? Do you find them amusing, sad, frustrating ... do you feel sorry for them, or angry with them?

9 Does the story make you feel that you might understand some old people better ... or perhaps understand why your own contemporaries act oddly at times?

An oppressive husband

A claustrophobic relationship of a different kind is revealed in 'Samphire'[2]. The story is economically told. Within half a page, we know how the husband sounds, and what the wife feels. It is the sound of his voice and her buried feelings that dominate the story. Like the previous story, we are most aware of a series of trivial moments that suggest the life of the couple. While there is a 'significant moment', it becomes more of an anticlimax, characteristic of the story's effect.

We are alerted to the husband's character by the nature of his repeated exclamations of excitement at discovering the samphire. Although it is told in the third person, we are allowed only to feel Molly's almost inarticulate anger: 'there was something in her throat so strong that she could not have spoken it if it had been for her life.' We are made to feel what it is like living with 'Lacey' by following him through several small incidents, where we hear him talk to various people. All the time, we are aware of the silent, brooding presence of Molly watching, hating.

Lacey's insecurity is revealed in his determination to present a particular public face; assuming social superiority over the coastguards, '"Good day, men"', and assuring the shopkeeper 'that they were not ordinary summer people'; his determination to claim credit for conquering Molly's fear of heights and his relentless satisfaction over discovering the samphire. The more sordid, hidden side comes over in 'his secret night-voice' and the invention of his own 'pet name'. The response of others to him suggests the impression he creates.

Molly does not speak at all in the story. She cannot perhaps trust herself to speak. She seems tense, repressed – a respectable background is hinted at in 'her uncle's church': we can only conjecture what has driven her into Lacey's arms. She wishes that at least he could see beauty in the samphire, not merely childish triumph. It is perhaps unfortunate that at the significant moment of the story, her action quickly turns to anticlimax. The moral weakness that prevents her from merely leaving Lacey, is reflected in physical weakness when she can no longer repress her horror at his overbearing behaviour, and tries to push him off the cliff, 'but as she pushed him she felt her arms weak like jelly'.

Rather like 'The Daughters of the Late Colonel', the story leaves us where it began, with life likely to resume as before. Lacey is already reinterpreting the incident as an accident, and Molly seems too to have grasped her fate, condemned to living with Lacey for ever. In both stories, the insufferable, dominant male characters have exerted too powerful an influence on those around them. Con, Jug and Molly are left with the inescapable consequences.

Consider the following:

1. Briefly list all the occasions on which Lacey meets other people, and note their reaction to him. How do they seem to feel about him?
2. Briefly list all the occasions on which he talks to Molly. What is revealed of the way he seems to see the relationship?
3. Do you think Molly is weak? Is she right to try to kill Lacey rather than, for instance, leaving him?
4. Explain these two phrases:
   'He had fallen off a cliff all right.'
   'She turned her dying face to the ground.'
5. Do you find the story depressing? If so, why?

Assignments

1 Compare what we discover about Colonel Pinner with what we know of Lacey. What similarities/differences are there between them? What is your personal feeling about them?

Suggested notes for essay answer:

Introduction: Both characters dominate those closest to them – Colonel Pinner more dominant – intimidates – Lacey seems more insecure – treated with disdain – contempt by others – only power over Molly.

Paragraph 2: Influence over daughters made clear – their timidity – fear of father – memory of eye glaring p. 104 – anxiety at burying father 'without asking his permission' – fear of finding him 'in the chest of drawers' – instinctive hurry to stop organ-grinder p. 121 – their indecision.

Paragraph 3: Influence too on others – Mr Farolles's panic at almost sitting in his chair p. 105 – Cyril's nervousness at meeting the Colonel pp. 116–17 – flashback shows brusque, impatient attitude – irritated etc.

Paragraph 4: Lacey's dominance solely over Molly – attempts to boost own ego – claims credit not only for discovery of samphire – but too for Molly conquering fear of heights – has to invent own 'pet name' – 'secret night-voice'.

Paragraph 5: Attempts to impress others fall flat – coastguards ignore him – tobacconist does not understand joke – man at hotel 'nodded' to Lacey's comments – insignificance.

Conclusion: Colonel Pinner more intimidating – Lacey more insecure – Colonel Pinner's irascibility genuinely daunting – Lacey's relentless egotism contemptible.

2 What similarities/differences do you find in the lives of Con and Jug compared with that of Molly? For whom do you feel most sympathy?

3 Re-read sections III and IX of 'The Daughters of the Late Colonel'. Write an account of a conversation between Mr Farolles and Colonel Pinner (with Con and Jug present making some contribution to the conversation).

4 Explain how Colonel Pinner's influence on his daughters is made clear. What are your feelings towards the daughters?

5 Much of the story is in dialogue – show how we learn more about three of the following characters through this approach: Colonel Pinner, Con, Jug, Cyril or Kate.

6 How much of our impression of Lacey is created through his dialogue?

7 Write a letter from Lacey to Molly's uncle giving an account of the holiday.

8 Compare what you feel are Molly's reasons for trying to kill Lacey, with Jackson's murder of Babyface in 'Late Night on Watling Street' and Soni's murder of his father in 'Drunkard of the River'. Are there any similarities or differences? Can any of these acts be justified?

9 Imagine Molly's and Lacey's future – write an episode from later in their life.

10 Both stories seem sad or even depressing. Have you enjoyed them as well? Can we gain anything from such stories? Do they help us understand others? Refer to other stories too in your answer (consider perhaps 'Daughters of the Vicar'[3] and the contrast between the response of Mary and Louise.)

English coursework: The Short Story

11 Write your own story of someone left to live with the consequences of a decision he or she has made, or an inherited situation. (A series of moments from a life, or a single incident? From a first or third person point of view? How many characters? Male or female – the 'victims' in these stories have been women. Can men be victims too? The importance of dialogue?)

Atmosphere through dialogue

Facing up to the past

The opening of Hemingway's 'The Killers'[9] is striking. Essentially through dialogue a sense of menace is established. Al and Max seem almost deliberately to misunderstand what they are told and take offence aggressively. '"What the hell do you put it on the card for?"', '"So you think that's right?"'. The peaceful conversation between Nick and George in a small diner, in a quiet American town, is disturbed by this suddenly threatening intrusion. Hemingway's terse and exact style creates a sharply focused scene.

We may be alerted to the status of Al and Max by the 'derby hat and black overcoat buttoned across the chest ... the silk muffler and gloves' they both wear. The tension increases as they tie up Nick and the cook, and openly accept that they are there to murder Ole Andreson, a Swede who lives in the town. As customers enter and are encouraged by George to leave, the two maintain their vigil – constant references to the slow passing of time contributing to the tension. In what is almost an anti-climax, Al and Max decide that Andreson will not arrive. Arbitrarily they decide not to shoot George and the others, despite knowing of the plan to murder the Swede.

Up to now, the story has created a tense atmosphere, but there has been little involvement with the characters. Like Al and Max we know nothing of the intended victim. Nick, the same observer, although older, as in 'Indian Camp'[2], determines to see Andreson. Their meeting alters the focus of the story. It now becomes a contrast between how the two face the consequences of what Nick has seen. It becomes perhaps a comparison of how death is faced by the younger and older man, by youth and age.

Ole Andreson has been living with the consequences of an

undisclosed act in his past for too long. All he will say to Nick is "'I got it wrong'". But he realizes that he cannot alter the situation: "'There isn't anything I can do about it.'" The police cannot help him. He has determined to face his fate, although poignantly: "'I just can't make up my mind to go out. I been in here all day.'" His acceptance of his inevitable death seems heroic. In contrast, Nick cannot face the prospect of staying in the town knowing of Andreson's intention.

While we are plunged into a dramatic situation in the story, it is dependent on a key moment that has already happened. For Nick too, this has become a significant experience, helping to test his own readiness to face death. Again, we are aware of an unwritten story behind the details that make up the actual story.

Consider the following:

1 List other moments in the dialogue of Al and Max where there seems a hint of threat towards those they address.
2 Would this story be equally successful if told in the first person by Nick?
3 List details which help to build up the tension in the story.
4 Why do you think Ole Andreson stays? Would you? Give your reasons.
5 Why does Nick plan to leave? Would you? Give your reasons.
6 Try to get hold of a copy of *In Our Time*, a collection of stories by Hemingway, with other stories where the observer is Nick. What is your impression of Nick's attitudes?

Assignments

1 Read 'Indian Camp'[2] and compare Nick's attitude to death in each. Do you think his earlier experience has influenced his attitude in 'The Killers'?
Suggested notes for essay answer:

Introduction: Distinction perhaps between a youthful and more aware view of life/death – Nick is older – has seen more by time of 'The Killers' – understands the realities more.

English coursework: The Short Story

Paragraph 1: In 'Indian Camp' Nick is young – naïve – wants to seem knowledgeable – 'I know . . . I see' – at the time is upset by woman's screams – his view of the dead Indian not qualified by comment – reaction comes afterwards – rowing to shore – contrasts with father's distress at what he's inflicted on Nick – Nick remains untouched 'quite sure that he would never die' – as if his innocence is confirmed by the experience.

Paragraph 2: Nick's experience in 'The Killers' also disturbing – frightening – tries to 'swagger it off' as he did on way to the Indian camp – experience of visit to Andreson prevents such an attempt – cannot live with Andreson's acceptance of his inevitable death – decides to leave town.

Conclusion: Nick's innocence protects him in 'Indian Camp' – the older Nick no longer able to stay untouched – death is now a reality – inevitable end that he is not yet ready to face.

2 Having read both stories, try to write a conversation in Hemingway's style between Nick and his father. Nick is trying to explain what he saw in the diner, and his conversation with Andreson and how he felt.

3 Both 'The Killers' and 'The Raid'[8] create tension. Compare the ways in which they achieve their effect.

4 Do you admire Ole Andreson? Why does he behave as he does?

5 Many other stories deal with characters facing the consequences of death in their lives. Compare their attitudes. (Consider stories from your own reading or try particularly 'Hunters and Hunted'[4], 'The Living'[8], 'Life of Ma Parker'[8], 'Odour of Chrysanthemums'[1,3].)

6 Write your own story of someone coming to terms with the consequences of a death. (Does the story have to be sad? Will it be based on a key moment?)

The Setting

Discussion in previous sections has concentrated on the narrative – on what happens – but the setting is often just as important in many stories. Some authors return constantly to their own personal background, their own experience being central to what they write – as in the case for instance of D. H. Lawrence, Alan Sillitoe or Bill Naughton. In such cases, the setting is often drab, depressing, and reflects the lives of those who live there. At other moments the setting can serve to help create the atmosphere of a story: the deserted, dark and windy streets of John Steinbeck's 'The Raid'[8] places emphasis on the edgy conversation of the two men, helping to create the tension at the centre of the story.

Other stories concentrate more on establishing the background against which characters move: the heat of the Southern states of the USA compared to the cold of the Northern states is central to Fitzgerald's story 'The Ice Palace'[2]. In 'Cane is Bitter'[4] by Samuel Selvon, the customs and traditions of the cane-cutting community are vividly presented so that we can better appreciate the conflict between the expectations of a more traditional society, with the possibilities offered by education which Romesh has to face. The setting of some stories depends on the interpretation of the main character, and in a story like Dylan Thomas's 'The Peaches'[2], on that of a child's sense of place and atmosphere.

An industrial landscape

The opening of D. H. Lawrence's 'Odour of Chrysanthemums'[1,3] shows how important the setting of a story is. The incident the story describes – the death of a miner in a mining accident – was relatively commonplace at the time, but cannot alter the significance of the death for those around him. Because a reader is separated from the incident both by time and, perhaps, by experience, it is an important part of the story's effect that it suggests to us what it was like living there at that time. The sense of industrial life – the locomotive serving the colliery, gradually taking over from the natural world – the colt 'that outdistanced it at a canter', is made apparent in a series of specific details.

Despite the colt's speed, this is a world in which nature is suffering on this 'raw afternoon' of 'stagnant light' where oak leaves are 'withered', fields are 'dreary and forsaken', and where industrial life has left its scars: 'The pit-bank loomed up beyond the pond, flames like red sores licking its ashy sides...' Yet the colliery also provides a livelihood for this community.

Within this perspective, the 'odour of chrysanthemums' takes on a distorted significance for Elizabeth Bates. Even the term 'odour' avoids any sense of fragrance. Lawrence uses the flowers as a symbol of her marriage with Walter; as his absence lengthens, she begins to consider the nature of their relationship. Her son's tearing at the chrysanthemums reminds her of her husband. The tenderness with which she places the flowers in her apron band (her daughter's delight in seeing them, emphasizing the unusual gesture) suggests a love that has been buried. 'It was chrysanthemums when I married him...', but also helps to suggest the physical fact of his death: 'One of the men had knocked off a vase of chrysanthemums.'

It is only within the world so sharply introduced to us in the first paragraph that the chrysanthemums, which 'hung dishevelled' among 'wintry primroses', can seem a significant symbol of a relationship. When we look closely at the details of the story, we might feel that Elizabeth – like the chrysanthemums – had also the potential to flower, but instead has withered, never quite coming to terms with the relationship with her husband until confronted by his death.

Consider the following:

1 Consider each of the various references to chrysanthemums – what do you think Elizabeth feels for her husband at each mention?

2 Much of the atmosphere of the story is also created by Elizabeth's growing awareness of her husband's late arrival and of her suspicions as to why he is late. Consider the various stages of her concern; when does her anger begin to turn to fear? What do we learn of their relationship in this initial stage of the story?

3 Were this story to open with a description of your own local

area, what further details would need to be changed to make it convincing? Would the basic details of the story be sufficient — what are the basic details?

Effects of sound and light

The first paragraph of Steinbeck's 'The Raid'[8] makes us aware of the darkness and silence of the small Californian town into which Dick and Root stride. The sense of darkness is heightened by the emphasis on the lights: the swinging of the blue arc lights on the street corners, reflected in dirty windows, a 'block tower up the line a little was starred with green lights', or the 'terrible light' of a train as it swept past. Instead of visual details of the town, we are made aware of its smell, 'the sweet smell of fermenting fruit'.

Sound too is emphasized: their 'footsteps echoed back loudly', Root's nervous whistling, the train which 'hooted mournfully'. We are aware of their tension as the first section comes to a close, and they become gradually engulfed by the darkness; we receive only hints as to the reason for their anxiety. As the story continues, the darkness and silence become increasingly the backcloth of their concern. In the darkness of a deserted store, the one kerosene lamp becomes the only light as they wait — either for those attending their meeting or for the raid they fear. Root imagines voices, but is mistaken as the night noises take over again.

The constant repetition of sounds of the wind, the dog barking, trains in the distance, all contribute to a sense of normality about to be broken. But the 'quick footsteps' we hear are of someone coming to warn them and our suspicions that the meeting they are to hold is not welcome is confirmed. It is characteristic that the eventual 'raid' is signalled by 'a rushing clatter of footsteps'. While the central conflict of the story may be a clash of beliefs, between those who do believe — here in Communism, though it seems more the courage behind any belief that interests Steinbeck — and those who will not listen, we are made to feel Dick and Root's courage through their nervousness. Already nervous, the darkness and silence of a strange town disturbs them, making them acutely conscious of what might erupt and influence their fate.

Consider the following:

1 When reading the story, are you more aware of the atmosphere, or the feelings of the two men? Do you feel that the atmosphere adds anything to how they feel?

2 Reading closely, are we made aware of a difference between their characters because of the way each responds differently to the atmosphere?

3 What other setting can you imagine for this story?

4 What impression would the story have made were the atmosphere that of your own local streets? Would the story be more convincing or less? Why?

Unfamiliar backgrounds

While all stories, to some extent, take us outside ourselves, the effect of some depend on our understanding a background of which we may have little experience. Three further stories introduce us to the very different cultures of Wales, the West Indies, and the USA. Each of the authors finds an individual way of representing his particular sense of place. While Dylan Thomas – better known as a poet – uses a young child's imagination to suggest an experience of Wales in 'The Peaches'[2], Scott Fitzgerald relies on the imagery of heat and cold to convey the distinctions between the Southern and Northern states of America. Samuel Selvon is concerned with a more realistic atmosphere – the sounds, smells and feelings of a small community in Trinidad just before cane cutting.

The Wales of 'The Peaches' is filtered through the young Dylan's thoughts and imagination, though it is told by an older Dylan looking back at his holiday as a boy. While we get a more vivid sense of the farm than we do of the Welsh setting, that setting becomes a significant part of the story's effect. Early in the story we get a sense of how the young Dylan's imagination can transform his surroundings. Tired and left in a dark passage while his uncle visits a pub, Dylan conjures up various nightmarish images and demons.

His perception of the farm is sharply observed, as we are gradually drawn into its decaying atmosphere. The details of its smell 'of rotten wood and damp and animals' that strike him at night become 'the sweetness of wood and the fresh green grass' after a night's sleep has revived him. But he is sufficiently clear-sighted to note the 'quiet, untidy farmyard', which is described in such detail on pp. 15–16. However, the imagination that can transform Uncle Jim into a fox 'tall and sly and red' can also inflate the wealth of his best friend's mother when she brings her son, Jack, to stay with Dylan.

The clash between the world of the farm and that of money is at the centre of the story. However hard Aunt Annie tries to disguise the state of the farm, its shabbiness becomes clear. The best room is ruthlessly pinned down, smelling of 'moth-balls and fur and damp and dead plants and stale, sour air'. Annie may change her dress but she forgets to change her gym shoes 'which were caked in mud and all holes'. The effect of the room on Mrs Williams is delicately observed: 'She dusted the seat of a chair with a lace handkerchief from her bag before sitting down.'

While Dylan is 'young and loud and alive' and his imagination continues to create stories around himself, the decaying farm and eccentricity of the characters cannot touch him. The spoilt Jack, however, sees the farm more clear-sightedly, is frightened of Gwilym, and resents Uncle Jim's threats. The setting of the farm – and the way in which it is differently perceived by Dylan and Jack – is an essential ingredient of the story.

Consider the following:

1 Consider the descriptions of the farm (e.g. pp. 15–16, 19–20). Which details suggest a small boy's observation, and which an older viewpoint – as it were, looking over the small boy's shoulder?

2 Rereading the story, what details suggest that it is set in Wales? Could it be set where you live? If not, what would need to be changed?

'The Ice Palace'[2] – already discussed in an earlier section ('A Significant Experience') – also relies on the sense of place that Fitzgerald creates in the distinctions between the climates of the Southern and the Northern states of America. We need only consider the first section where the effect of the constant sunshine is reflected in the behaviour of the inhabitants: terms like 'profound inertia', 'pleasant langour', 'languid paradise' are common, while even the buildings carry the burden of the heat, the Happer house facing the street 'with a tolerant, kindly patience', and shops seem near to 'retiring into a state of utter and finite coma'. The contrast with Harry Bellamy from the North is crisply made: he is described as 'tall, broad and brisk'.

Samuel Selvon's 'Cane is Bitter'[4] opens with a description of the community to which the central character, Romesh, returns. It is important that we, as readers, should grasp the nature and feelings of this community so that we can better understand, and perhaps see with his eyes, both the attractions and the limitations of their insular world. Those who have been given education cannot help but see the world in a different way.

The community we are introduced to is shown as happy, expectant – with the prospect of work and money that cane-cutting introduces, and traditional in the expectations of male and female roles. We are made aware of the burning straw, 'the black straw which rose on the wind', and of the laughter of the children as they smear themselves with the black streaks from the straw, or play in the muddy pond among mothers washing clothes or fathers washing 'mules and donkeys and hog-cattle'. There is the unity of a close-knit community.

It is only as the story focuses on the characters of Romesh's parents against the vivid picture of the village that we realize something of the expectations of this culture. Their expectations conflict – between what education might provide, and what tradition expects. While Rookmin is optimistic that education might lead to wealth – if Romesh becomes a doctor or lawyer – Ramlal's vision is more determined by traditional ideas such as an arranged marriage. They do not realize that, having given Romesh the opportunity of education, they no longer have a choice.

The setting of the story – in the first two pages – allows us to share with Romesh the attractions of a world he knows he must leave behind: 'He knew that these were things not easily forgotten which he had to forget.' The world of Rookmin and Ramlal offers warmth and security but 'nothing would change ... No schooling, no education, no widening of experience ...'. He can cope with the experience only by losing himself in the competition of his youth – challenging Hari to a cane-cutting contest.

Once he understands what is mapped out for him, marriage with Doolsie, within a world of 'tradition and custom', his decision is made. He knows now that life has more to offer; he makes a final gesture in helping to win the bonus for his family, but will return to the world that he feels offers more potential ... The strength of his feelings is heightened by the fact that we learn of the attractions of the close-knit community of which he has been a part; we learn little detail of his education. Already though, he is an outsider ...

Assignments

1 In 'Cane is Bitter', would we understand Romesh as well without the description of his village at the beginning of the story? What insights into the conflict between himself and his family are shown by the early description?

Suggested notes for essay answer:

Introduction: Story partly about impact of education on traditional culture – also about personal tensions this creates – to feel this as reader, must be aware of world in which these tensions emerge.

Paragraph 1: Opening paragraphs suggest harmony – happiness – prospect of work – money – traditional sense of male/female roles – awareness of children's laughter – but too an unrelenting life – Ramlal 'dedicated to wrestling an existence for herself and her family' – opening conversation deepens sense of importance of tradition – suspicion of education within community.

Paragraph 2: Romesh's previous visit alerted family to changes in him – he perceives dangers of 'ignorance and the wasting away of their lives' – 'accepting our fate like animals' – but within their own insular world, can only see solution of the arranged marriage – power of custom – win Romesh back.

Paragraph 3: Romesh has hardened himself against the attractions of his past – the evocative smells and sounds of his youth – participation in cane-cutting does not signify a return – mention of arranged marriage sparks off conflict between potential of education and tradition – his decision – 'revolt against parents' wishes, against tradition and custom'.

Conclusion: Necessary that we feel the pull of village customs –

the lure of the past – to understand change in Romesh – the pain that accompanies growing up – education – possibility of choice.

2 Comparing the stories discussed in this section, which setting makes most impression on you? Which do you find most difficult to imagine? (Look closely at the details of the description in your answer.)

3 Considering at least two of the stories here, what effect do you think the setting of the story has on the main character(s)?

4 Read other stories by D. H. Lawrence – do others rely to the same extent as 'Odour of Chrysanthemums' on the setting of the story?

5 Compare 'The Raid' with 'The Killers': what sense of 'setting' do we get in 'The Killers'? (What sort of town is it? What clues make this clear to us? How does this affect the characters in it? Why has Ole Andreson come to this town?) What similarities and differences do you find between the two stories?

6 Do you consider the setting of 'The Peaches' more important or the way the young Dylan describes what he sees? Why? (Or compare 'My Oedipus Complex'[6] – is the personality of each child more important or what each sees?)

7 Taking any two of the stories, imagine yourself in the setting of the story. What changes would have to be made to make the story convincing?

8 Write a story in which you are the main character in any of the settings of the stories considered in this section *or* Write a story in which any of the characters in the stories considered in this section are seen against the setting of your own local area.

9 Write a story in which the setting is essential to the way the character(s) behave. (Is it the place – drab, beautiful, familiar, the atmosphere – sounds, smells, light/dark, or the physical reality – the weather, heat, or habitat or any combination of these that is going to make the main impression?)

10 What other stories have you read where you think the setting is of great importance, where a great deal of the story's significance lies in the background? Consider particularly stories of cultures that are unfamiliar to your own. Is the impression you gain sufficiently vivid to convince you of its existence? Explain why, looking closely at the details of the description.

Humanity and Nature

Some stories depend for their effect on the relationship between humanity and Nature. In such cases, the setting of the story is often particularly significant. For this kind of story to succeed, we need to be aware of the natural landscape behind the human characters. The conflict at the centre of such stories is often the struggle between the characters and the world around them, the need for humanity to dominate the natural world of which they are only a part. Humanity's 'victory' over the natural world is seen frequently as a hollow victory, revealing more about our weaknesses than our strengths.

Unequal struggles

In 'The Wedge-Tailed Eagle'[2], the reader is drawn quickly into the story from the first sentence: '... there is always something beside the sun watching you from the sky'; the use of 'you' forces the reader too to 'look'. The first paragraph focuses our attention on the 'hot, cloudless days' and the place of 'a black dot ... the circling eagle' within them. The second paragraph introduces the pilots stationed in New South Wales during the Second World War. They are aware of the effortless superiority of the eagle's natural ability in the air, compared with the mechanical efficiency of their own aeroplanes. The conflict between natural and mechanical, between what is freely enjoyed and what is made, is at the centre of the story.

Where human society has encroached on the natural world, the original inhabitants can seem a threat. Where the pilots appreciate the eagle's qualities, 'the most magnificent, majestic bird there is', the farmer sees him purely as a scavenger, a threat to his livelihood. Ironically it is precisely the majesty of the eagle that becomes threatening to the pilots, who regard themselves as masters of the air.

In 'Hunters and Hunted'[4] (considered more fully in 'A Significant Experience'), the hunters are fully aware of the dangers of nature. The reader is made aware too by the initial description of the 'Black Bush', the swamp, 'tall trees, massed growths of bamboo and closely woven tapestries of vines and creepers';

within this jungle, the wild pigs' attack on the jaguar leaves no doubt as to the power of the natural world within its own environment. Again the appreciation of Doorne and his sons of this natural world is balanced by their determination to invade it for their own gain. They pay a heavy price.

In 'The Rain Horse'[2], a 'young man' returns to a landscape from his past. From the first sentence we are aware of the rain that becomes a major part of the story's effect. The writer of the story, Ted Hughes, is better known as a poet. The first sentence of the second paragraph, 'He had come too far', could merely be a factual statement, but as so often in poetry, the statement seems to carry a significance beyond itself. He is not dressed for a raw, wet day; the suit and shoes he wears are those of a stranger, and they have been wrecked as he strays further into a hostile environment which – twelve years on – he no longer understands: 'shallow, bare fields, black and sodden as the bed of an ancient lake after the weeks of rain.'

In each of the three stories, men pit themselves against a natural world that we are made almost physically to feel – whether the cloudless morning, the sky 'endlessly stretching, magnificent in freedom', or the pull of the swamp as Tonic 'staggered ... forced his way through bisi-bisi and wild cane reeds', or the relentless pounding of the rain, 'the plastering beat of icy rain on his bare skull'. At the centre of each story is the moment of conflict between the men and some force from nature – the eagle, the bush hogs, and the rain horse. In each case it is nature that has the last word.

In 'The Wedge-Tailed Eagle', the pilots do appreciate the eagle's 'inborn mastery' but their vanity – and perhaps their immaturity – forces them to challenge it. They see it as a contest, with the risk of death equally shared between themselves and the eagle. It is only with their 'victory' that they begin to understand the reality of a contest imposed by them, or the inevitable nature of any 'victory' they could win.

For Doorne and his sons, hunting is a necessity, part of their culture, and important for economic reasons. They also appreciate the dangers of the forest in which they hunt. Only Tonic, for whom this is a kind of initiation into family ways, is unaware of the reality with which he is involved. His exuberance causes the careless slip that leads to his death.

A real or imagined struggle?

The young man in 'The Rain Horse'[2] no longer understands the landscape of his youth. He has changed. The landscape is no longer that 'pleasantly remembered'. His hopes of finding something of his youth, 'something, some pleasure, some meaningful sensation, he didn't quite know what,' have disappeared; he feels resentful, 'so outcast, so old and stiff and stupid' that his only desire is to escape. It is at this point that something 'meaningful' does erupt from nature, something threatening and 'nightmarish'.

The subsequent attacks from the 'rain horse', from this world he no longer understands, become linked with his journey into his past. In his attempt to come to terms with his past he has strayed 'too far'; he has come seeking an artificially 'significant' experience but meets a physical experience that suggests the potential danger of Nature. Perhaps too, the young man is warned about the dangers of trying to meddle with a past that can also seem remote and threatening.

While the eagle and bush hogs are suggested as purely physical presences, particularly as the eagle crashes to the ground, the rain horse seems to fulfil two purposes. In one sense it too is a terrifying physical presence, the ground shaking at its approach, the detail of its emergence (see pp. 59, 61 and 63), 'the crack of the impact' as it is struck by the stone. In some ways, however, we are encouraged to feel that the horse is imaginary; at one moment 'its whinnying snort and the splattering whack of its hooves seemed to be actually inside his head', and with its disappearance something is 'cut from his brain'. Ted Hughes perhaps uses the horse in a dual capacity, as a real eruption from Nature, but symbolically too, for the thoughts and feelings of the past which in reality he does not wish to face – like the horse, 'Keep your distance and you'll not get hurt'.

Consider the following:

1 Why do you think the pilots decide to attack the eagle? Consider carefully the paragraph on p. 32 that describes 'A pilot'.

2 Read the last page of the story carefully. What kind of 'victory' does the dead eagle represent? Why do the pilots bury the

English coursework: The Short Story

eagle? Why do they run to avoid the farmer at the end of the story?

3 Whose view of the eagle do you more readily accept, that of the farmer or the pilots? Is there a further view that they fail to consider?

4 Make a brief list of phrases that suggest the air and land in which 'The Wedge-Tailed Eagle' is set, and a further list that describes the landscape of 'Hunters and Hunted'. Which strikes you as the most vivid? Why?

5 Make a list of the descriptions of the rain in 'The Rain Horse'. Do they seem repetitive, or is there a distinction between them?

6 Does 'The Rain Horse' confuse you? Do you know what it is about? What effects stay with you at the end of the story?

7 What is your impression of the young man in the story? Do you feel any sympathy for him in his fear of the horse, or does he merely panic?

Assignments

1 Imagine that you are the farmer from 'The Wedge-Tailed Eagle'. Write a letter to a neighbouring farmer, who also regards the eagle as a menace, describing the events of the story. (Include your initial impression of the pilots, how you regard their skill, any feelings you might have about their hasty exit at the end of the story, as well as the details of the 'battle'.)

Suggested notes for essay answer:

Paragraph 1: Finally got rid of that stinking, great carcass of an eaglehawk – fed up with it feeding off my sheep – wondered if you wanted an idea of how to deal with your pair – hire the Air Force!

Paragraph 2: Peculiar story really – met couple of pilots from the new station – having couple of drinks – they'd seen the eagles – impressed by them – don't know why – told them of my problem – mind you, their plane's not much bigger than that eagle! – they reckoned two planes could do it – I reckoned it was the drink talking.

Paragraph 3: Couple of days later – hear plane low over the valley – see one of them – waved – perfect weather for them – cloudless – hot – must admit, he could fly that plane – only a few feet above the ground – then, saw the bird – other pilot was high in sky – obviously had planned to get it.

Paragraph 4: Though not an admirer of that eagle – had to laugh at first – outflew those planes with ease – not remotely concerned – then they trapped it – forced bird into position into which other plane was diving – still escaped but looked more anxious – next time they got it right – this time second plane came from beneath – eagle flew straight into it – took off his wing just right – crash and down he came.

Paragraph 5: Had to hand it to them – great flying – and got rid of that bird – funny thing though – drove over to tell them what a good job they'd done – must have seen me – I waved – but they ran over to corner of paddock – buried corpse under some rocks – I'd have left it to rot – then they flew off – can't understand it – I want to buy them a drink . . .

and/or

Write a letter from the young man of 'The Rain Horse' to a friend of his who has also left the same home area. Using the details of the story, describe your experiences of that day. (Include your (vague) reasons for wanting to re-visit, the disappointment you felt, the details of the weather, how you felt when you were attacked, and your final feelings of the day.)

2 Do your feelings towards the pilots in 'The Wedge-Tailed Eagle' change in the course of the story? (Consider their reasons for attacking the eagle, and their reaction at the end, as well as what we learn about them, and their attitude to the 'battle'.)

3 Do you believe the horse in 'The Rain Horse' to be real or imaginary, or are you unsure? Give reasons for your answer. Does the nature of the horse make any difference to your impression of the story?

4 Each of the three stories deals with creatures confident in their own environment. Looking closely at how they are described, and their effect in each story, compare the conclusion you reach about the creatures in each story. Which frightens you the most?

English coursework: The Short Story

5 Compare closely the descriptions of the natural landscapes in each of the stories. Which appears to you the most vividly described? Try to account for your reasons.

6 Do you feel that any of the men in these stories is justified in the attitude he takes to Nature (including the creatures within it)?

7 Do any of these stories make you angry about the way the characters behave? Try to account for your feelings.

8 Are there any moments in your life when something in the natural world has frightened or disturbed you? Write an account of the incident, including both the factual details and your feelings. *or* Write a story in which the central character(s) confront(s) something within a natural landscape that you have established in some detail. (Consider his/her/their feelings before and after the confrontation.)

A symbolic struggle

A further story that deals with the relationship between humanity and Nature does so in a quite different way. 'Lie thee down, Oddity'[2] is most difficult to 'pin down', but perhaps because it is more open to discussion, seems particularly satisfying. The further into the story we read the clearer it becomes that this is not a 'realistic' story. It is symbolic – in that the deeds and gestures of Mr Cronch represent his approach to life rather than what would necessarily happen in real life.

Throughout the story, we are made to feel the contrast between 'wild, fierce, untutored' nature, and the way in which humanity tries to control it, to tame it into 'the soft pelt of a smooth lawn'. This contrast (pp. 110–11, 113, 115, 118) helps to explain the difference between Mr Cronch and others. Although Nature has a cruel, ruthless side, like a 'savage animal' (consider the ravens, p. 115), it seems closer to more essential values of life: 'when darkness came it was the darkness of God.'

The lawn becomes a symbol of how in 'civilized' society, natural elements in life are tamed, and humanity retreats to a reduced, more artificial world, living for instance in towns, accepting the reduced quality of vegetables that wouldn't find a buyer in the country (see pp. 117–18). Eventually, life becomes

Humanity and Nature

conventional and easy, and moral judgements slide too as we lose contact with the direct challenge of Nature.

While we do not feel the direct, physical sense of nature as vividly here as in the other stories, we are never allowed to lose sight of its ruthlessness ('The ravens flew off and looked for a lamb to kill'). Mr Cronch merely sees in Nature a more direct way of dealing with problems in life: he sees further perhaps than the other characters in this chapter. He is prompted to face the challenges of life more directly by the 'Oddity'. He is not prepared merely to accept an easy life. He has always used simple, direct methods even as a gardener: even the mower 'might ... have been used by Adam'. Leaving his comfortable world, he takes a cottage on the wild heath, confronting the elements of nature, attempting to 'reclaim the garden' – perhaps symbolically an attempt to forge a new Eden through his individual effort, his strength, his example.

Such a task demands more than battling with the wilderness; having cultivated the heath, 'the Oddity would not lie down', and Mr Cronch embarks on a series of battles with need and despair. Like his Oddity, his need to do what is right is not conventional, nor are his solutions – when faced with the man for whom nothing can be done and who desires death, he merely helps him by pushing him into the river. The policeman's response to this is not 'realistic' – '"You will appear at court, charged with murder ... But now you may go!"' – merely serving to show how conventional society disapproves of what seems to Mr Cronch a more honest treatment of the man's predicament. Finally he shows courage and reassurance literally 'in the shadow of death', his hat another form of symbol of his fight against distress or despair.

Few men wear their hat as fittingly as Mr Cronch. Unwilling to settle for a safe, secure world of conventional judgements, such men face direct, difficult decisions and administer them impartially rather as decisions are made in the natural world.

Consider the following:

1 Briefly list the various episodes in which Mr Cronch is involved (from pp. 114–120) and consider how most people would have responded to the various people he meets. Do you agree with his solutions to the various problems?

2 What do you believe the 'Oddity' was?

3 What significance was there in his hat?

4 Did you enjoy this story or do you prefer more 'realistic' stories? Give your reasons.

5 What is your final impression of Mr Cronch?

Assignments

1 How does the world of the 'wild heath' compare with the images of nature considered in other stories of this section? (You will need to consider the detail of the various descriptions.)
Suggested notes for essay answer:

Introduction: Various stories use 'nature' in different ways – some make us more aware of physical reality – humanity's attempt to impress itself – cannot be 'tamed' – others see nature as an important symbol – the wild – savage – challenge to 'civilized' values – as with 'wild heath'.

Paragraph 1: Stories like 'the Wedge-Tailed Eagle'/'Hunters and Hunted' create vivid sense of place – imagery stresses emptiness of sky – heat – or physical difficulty of moving through forest – both stress confidence/brutality of creatures within their environment – effortless superiority of eagle – savagery of wild hogs.

Paragraph 2: 'The Rain Horse' also makes us vividly aware of landscape – particularly through description of rain – of rain horse – terrifying eruption – but too symbol of distance between now urban main character and his 'roots' – a natural world.

Paragraph 3: 'wild heath' of 'Lie thee down, Oddity' still more symbolic – represents untamed/savage side of living – ignored in 'civilized' society – metaphorical (an indirect comparison) – 'It was a savage animal' – not a real world – one in which the wild still thrives – 'The wild birds had rest' – less important to feel its physical reality – becomes the validity for Mr Cronch's moral decisions.

Conclusion: 'wild heath' shares some qualities with rain horse – has symbolic value beyond realistic – but we are made to feel purely the power of nature more vividly in other stories.

2 Do you admire Mr Cronch's behaviour or do you find it unsympathetic? In what situations do you believe you would wish to be helped by him? (Refer in detail to the story in your answer.)

3 Both 'The Rain Horse' and 'Lie thee down, Oddity', contain 'symbolic' elements that are an important part of their final effect – how effective do you find such stories compared to 'realistic' ones? (Refer to details like the rain horse, the Oddity, or the hat, for instance.)

4 Read 'Growing Up'[2], and particularly the description of the 'wilderness' at the beginning. How do you think the wilderness has affected the children's behaviour?

5 Compare Mr Cronch with Mr Quick. How do you think they would regard each other's behaviour? (Begin by comparing your impression of each, based on their behaviour and on the incidents in which they are involved.)

6 Write an account of a girl or woman in conflict with Nature. (Would their response be different to that of the men here – more sensible, less combative? Importance of setting? Written from first person or third person point of view? A key moment or series of incidents?)

Humour

Many stories make us laugh. It is never easy to explain quite why. A sense of humour varies from person to person. It releases tensions; it is often a shared feeling that pulls people together. It is clear that the stories considered in this section will not make everyone laugh – or perhaps they will laugh for different reasons – but they may make trying to define our own individual sense of humour easier. Few, for instance, would find 'Samphire'[2] (considered in more detail in 'Living with the Consequences') funny, but we may find 'Lacey' so grotesque, so appalling, as to be laughable.

Escaping reality

Much humour relies on the exaggeration of human traits common to most of us. We all daydream. Walter Mitty in 'The Secret Life of Walter Mitty'[2] daydreams constantly to escape the realities of his life. The opening of the story can seem confusing, but we are thrown straight into one of his fantasies. We may find humour in the way he always finds himself in impossible situations, but he is always the hero finding a way out. We may find humour in the contrast between his real life – henpecked by his bossy, maternal wife – and the fantasies in which he takes on the dominant role.

The structure of the story is simple. We follow Walter Mitty through a morning's shopping. Prompted by the different activities in which he finds himself – driving, parking, shopping, or waiting for his wife – he loses himself in a different fantasy. In each case, he is rudely awakened from his daydream by the new situation his imagination has landed him in, whether driving into a car park in the exit lane, or finding an irritated Mrs Mitty searching for him.

The absurdity of the situations in which he finds himself can be a source of humour, for example, his mending the hugely complicated new anaesthetizer by replacing a faulty piston with a fountain pen: "'That will hold for ten minutes ... Get on with the operation.'" There is often an element of painful truth contained within humour however. All of Mitty's fantasies are based on the most clichéd scenes of pulp fiction or film; even in his fantasies he cannot be truly independent. There is something pathetic in his clinging to such images when he has not the courage to face real life. He cuts a poor figure, – 'A woman who was passing laughed...', and even the revolving doors 'made a faintly derisive whistling sound'. On the other hand, his habit does enable him eventually to cope at least with the life he has to live, 'Undefeated, inscrutable to the last.'

Consider the following:

1 How many fantasies are we presented with in this story? Are there similarities in the way each is presented?

2 What impression do we gain of Walter Mitty from those moments in which we see him in real life? Consider each moment closely.

3 What influence do you think Mrs Mitty has had on Walter?

4 Try to account for the repetitive mention of the 'pocketa-pocketa-pocketa' sound.

5 Did you find the story – or moments within it – funny? Why? What do you think this suggests about your sense of humour?

Through the eyes of a child

A self-interested child

The humour of some stories depends mostly on the way in which characters see the world about them. Children in particular often interpret the adult world from their own perspective, without ever really understanding why adults behave as they do. Larry, in 'My Oedipus Complex'[6], has found war (the First World War) to be 'the most peaceful period of my life' – being the centre of his mother's attention while his father is away in the war.

He is clearly a precocious child – and the way the story is told, by an older Larry looking back through the eyes of the younger, helps to make him seem older and more sure of himself. The vocabulary and sophistication often seem that of an adult, though his understanding is that of a child. For instance, while he believes his mother's suggestion that babies cost 17/6 (about 85p), he still concludes that 'that showed how simple she was' because another, poorer family – the Geneys – who could not afford that sum, still managed to have a new baby. 'It was probably a cheap baby, and Mother wanted something really good, but I felt she was too exclusive.'

At the centre of this story – the centre too of its humour – is the clash of personalities between Larry and his father, conducted in a series of skirmishes as they both attempt to win the attention of Larry's mother. As Larry is very sure of his own attraction, he can only assume that his father is using unfair weapons: 'It was clear that she either genuinely liked talking to father ... or else that he had some terrible hold on her.' With a child's logic, his response is to ask his mother '"Do you think if I prayed hard God would send Daddy back to the war?"'

After battles over the possession of the 'big bed', his father's toys – souvenirs from the war – and his 'unfair' advantage of reading to Larry's mother, peace returns ironically only with the birth of the new baby Larry so badly wanted. With all attention now concentrating on the baby, both Larry and his father are ignored, culminating in Larry's comment, '"If another bloody baby comes into this house, I'm going out."' The success of the story depends on Larry's assumption of his superiority to the adults in the story, despite revealing himself as the child he clearly is in his understanding of events.

Consider the following:

1 What impression does Larry make on you?

2 Do you think his father behaves childishly, or do you think there are other reasons for the way he behaves?

3 How well do you think Larry's mother deals with the jealousy between Larry and his father?

4 Did you find the story – or aspects of it – funny? Try to determine what amused you and why. (Try reading 'The Genius'[6] – is this funny in the same way?)

5 Read 'The Duke's Children'[6], much of which is comic – but the ending is slightly painful. Basically concerned with himself, Larry fails to understand Nancy's position. Do you think good humour requires an edge of sadness or reality?

A child's use of tactics

Nicholas, in 'The Lumber Room'[1], is also aware that on occasions adults behave as if they are 'older, wiser and better people' when clearly they are not. He sets out to prove the point by refusing to eat 'his wholesome bread-and-milk on the seemingly frivolous ground that there was a frog in it', a fact he knows to be true as he has placed it there himself. The description of him as a 'skilled tactician' becomes significant in the conflict at the centre of the story between Nicholas and his 'self-styled aunt'. No longer convinced of her superiority, he engages in a series of manoeuvres designed to outwit her.

The humour in the story depends on our sympathizing with Nicholas; we are encouraged to do so by the author's attitude towards the narrow, repressed and cheerless aunt, all of whose plans in the story revolve around the punishment of Nicholas. Having tricked her into believing that he wants to be in the gooseberry garden, he knows that she will place herself on 'self-imposed sentry-duty', allowing him to pursue his real purpose: the lumber room. The climax of the story finds the aunt trapped in a rain-water tank in the gooseberry garden, pleading with Nicholas to release her. To his great satisfaction he is able to use her own words against her, but characteristically does so with restraint.

The humour is often ironic (things seem to develop in the opposite way to that intended) in the story – in that very often the opposite to what the aunt plans actually happens. Looking for 'a few decent tears' from Nicholas (the notion of 'decent' tears suggesting the aunt's moral attitude) as the others leave for the beach, in fact 'all the crying was done by his girl-cousin who scraped her knee rather painfully . . .' The story works as a series of twists, in which the tactics of Nicholas outwit the expectations of the aunt.

Consider the following:

1 Write about the 'tactics' Nicholas uses throughout the story.

2 Make a list of phrases about or spoken by the aunt – what do they suggest about her?

3 Read the passage on pp. 92–3, from 'A few decent tears' to

English coursework: The Short Story

'said the aunt loftily.' What is revealed of each of them in this exchange?

4 In the final confrontation (pp. 96–7, from 'Nicholas, Nicholas!'), how does Nicholas manage to revenge himself on his aunt? (Look closely at the way he replies to her comments.)

5 Do you feel any sympathy for the aunt?

6 Compare Nicholas with Larry in 'My Oedipus Complex' – who is the more 'skilled tactician'? Who do you like most?

7 List the occasions on which the opposite to what the aunt has planned actually occurs.

A child's curiosity

A very different story – with a far blacker edge to the humour – is Alan Sillitoe's 'On Saturday Afternoon'⁷. A summary of the story, a man's attempt to kill himself, suggests that there is unlikely to be anything to amuse us. Again though, because the witness of the attempted suicide is a child, with little understanding of the adult world that has caused the man's situation, his observations do perhaps strike us as bleakly humorous. The opening paragraph establishes the tone of the boy's account. 'I once saw a bloke try to kill himself ... I was only a kid at the time, so you can imagine how much I enjoyed it.'

The world of this story is very different from that of 'The Lumber Room' as is clear from the colloquial way in which the main character speaks. From a deprived and more depressed background, a possible suicide strikes him as a situation at least as interesting as a visit to the cinema, an opportunity not to miss. Having learned of the man's intention, the boy follows him into the house, watching his preparations with a practical and at times enthusiastic interest – which becomes comically inappropriate. He remarks (and later repeats) "'It wain't hold up, mate'", as the man ties the rope to the light fitting. He readily agrees to kick the chair away on which the man is standing, and as he places the rope around his neck, is concerned to get a closer look at the impressive knot.

When the man is ready, the boy kicks away the chair as he promised: '[I] ... took a runner at it as if I was playing centre forward for Notts Forest and the chair went scooting back against the sofa'; at this point however, the light-fitting does indeed give way, and the man crashes to the floor. The humour then revolves around the boy's disappointment, '... hands stuffed deep into my pockets and nearly crying at the balls-up he'd made of everything.'

The twist in the story – as so often with Sillitoe – focuses on the police response. Attempted suicide was then a criminal offence. In hospital with a police guard, the man eventually does kill himself by throwing himself out of the window. 'It was marvellous though, the way the brainless bastards had put him in a ward six floors up, which finished him off proper...' In one sense, this is obviously a tragic story, but Sillitoe is more interested in how the boy sees the incident – the humour lies mainly in the boy's inability to grasp its significance. The bleakness of the background to the story remains, perhaps heightened by the story's approach.

Consider the following:

1 Do you feel that this story could be considered humorous? Say in what ways you find it so (if you do).

2 Would this be less successful if told in the third person?

3 What impression do we get of the boy? (Briefly list his observations on his father, the attempted suicide, the police.)

4 How does the boy here compare with Larry or Nicholas from the stories previously considered?

5 How would you describe Sillitoe's general outlook on the world in which the boy lives? (List some phrases used to describe the area in which he lived.)

6 How does the way in which the boy expresses himself help to establish his character?

7 Read Bill Naughton's 'The Key of the Cabinet'[5] or 'Poison Pincher'[5] – what similarities and differences do you find between these and 'On Saturday Afternoon' in the way the stories are written, the places in which they are set, and in the personalities of the narrators?

Assignments

1 Compare the various fantasies in which Walter Mitty loses himself. Looking at his behaviour in real life too, what do the fantasies tell us about Walter?

2 Invent a further moment in the story that stimulates another daydream. Explain where you would insert this episode, and include a reference to the 'pocketa-pocketa' sound.

3 What is your impression of Walter Mitty and Mrs Mitty? Do you have sympathy for either?

4 Write a story in which a wife takes refuge in daydreams to deal with her husband's dominance. (How would the story have to change? Would you start with the husband's behaviour, or the wife's daydreams? Would the nature of her daydreams be diferent from those of Walter Mitty?)

5 Looking closely at the way the story is told, how are we given the impression that Larry is older and more sophisticated than he actually is? How does this contribute to the humour?

6 Read 'The Genius'[6] and compare it to 'My Oedipus Complex' – what impression do we gain of Larry's personality from the two stories?

7 Having read these two stories, write Larry's diary – two or three entries, about the difficulties of living at home given his 'special' personality.

8 Compare others of Frank O'Connor's 'autobiographical' stories – while Larry can be engaging, what other aspects of his personality emerge?

9 Write a letter from Nicholas's aunt in 'The Lumber Room' to a close friend about Nicholas's behaviour. *or* Write a letter from Nicholas to a close friend, explaining his successful plan to outwit his aunt.

10 Do Nicholas's thoughts in the lumber room – particularly about the firescreen – reveal anything other than what is revealed in the rest of the story?

11 By comparing the background and style of 'The Lumber Room' and 'On Saturday Afternoon', what social differences can you find between them? Do any details allow us to draw conclusions about the period in which they are set?

12 What is funny – if anything – about 'On Saturday Afternoon'?

13 What impression do you gain of the boy in 'On Saturday Afternoon'? Write a description of the whole incident and his feelings about it.

14 Compare the ways in which Larry and Nicholas might have responded to the man's attempted suicide.

15 Compare any two of the stories considered here with one of your own choice. By looking closely at the detail of the stories, try to suggest which you find most amusing and why.

16 Had Nicholas, Larry or the boy in 'On Saturday Afternoon' been girls instead, would any of the three stories need to be changed in any way?

17 Write a humorous story in which a young girl or boy responds unexpectedly to an incident which in real life would be serious. (Use a first-person narrator; how will you establish their personality? How many other characters are there? Will you lead up to the 'significant moment', or will there be a series of incidents? What is the importance of setting/period?)

18 Write a humorous story in which things turn out in the opposite way to what was expected.

Style

The term 'style' is used positively here to describe the distinctions between the language used by different writers. The way in which an author writes is inevitably an important aspect. There is a vast difference between the style of Fitzgerald in 'The Ice Palace' for instance, and that of Hemingway in 'Indian Camp'. While Fitzgerald's language is rich, lush, suggestive, Hemingway's is spare, terse, with short sentences and few adjectives. Others may rely more on imagery, or symbolism, or sometimes dialogue may be central to the story's effect. Some writers deliberately use colloquial language to suggest a specific background to the story.

Imagery

It is characteristic of the writing in 'The Ice Palace'[2] that the sunlight 'dripped' in the first sentence. Towards the end of the first section, we read that the heat 'flowed ... like a great warm nourishing bosom for the infant earth'. A sense of dependence on the heat is established by the image. The use of comparisons – metaphors and similes – is extended to descriptions of cold: 'There was no sky – only a dark, ominous tent that draped in the tops of the streets and was in reality a vast approaching army of snowflakes.' We might question the idea of the tent that transforms itself into an army, but the comparisons help to suggest how the inhabitants are enveloped by the climate – the very reason that Sally-Carrol has to escape the claustrophobic atmosphere of the North. Fitzgerald uses the images to fix a vivid sense of the differences between the North and South of the United States.

When we read 'The Wedge-Tailed Eagle'[2], we are similarly struck by the use of images. Here they are used to reinforce the identity of the pilots who seek to compete with the eagle. These are men used to risk, accustomed to fighting with bullets and shells, thus the terms in which they see their world are defined by the terms of battle: 'The sky was as clean as a gun-barrel.' If a cloud appears in the empty sky, then it 'looks like a patch of rust in a gun-barrel'. Other images in the story are drawn from the mechanics of the aeroplane itself. Such a use of imagery keeps before us both a sense of the characters, and of the conflict itself, with its constant 'risk of death' on which the pilots appear to thrive.

Simplicity

It is the simplicity of Hemingway's 'Indian Camp'[2] that is more likely to catch our attention. The opening three paragraphs are notable for their lack of any device that might distract our concentration from the scene itself. We see all that Hemingway feels is necessary. A series of short sentences, constructed with a high proportion of monosyllabic words, deftly establishes the opening situation. The starkness of the style succeeds in focusing our attention intensely on each moment – having arrived at the camp, we are told: 'Inside on a wooden bunk lay a young Indian woman.' The story will revolve around the young woman lying on the bunk; in this paragraph and the following (the last two paragraphs on p. 147), we are told all we need to know about the conditions in which they live, to understand the reason for the eventual tragedy.

Because Hemingway strips away so much that we often associate with writers – adjectives, images, description, explanation, comment – it is true that the reader may seem to have to work harder. Reading becomes more of an act of collaboration with the writer. He does not help the reader for instance by trying to define the intonation or expression in dialogue; more often the most we are told is 'he said'. Here though, such lack of 'help' may point us towards Nick's uncertainty: '"Oh," said Nick ... "I see," Nick said.' In 'The Killers'[9], on the other hand, the lack of definition over the first two pages or so of dialogue serves to heighten the menace of Al and Max. We can hear the threat in the words they use without having to be told.

Another kind of simplicity can be achieved, as Ted Hughes does in 'The Rain Horse'[2], through the use of harsher, more emphatic language that owes more to an earlier tradition of English, its rhythms throwing emphasis on the significant aspects of the description. 'Now the valley lay sunken in front of him, utterly deserted, shallow bare fields, black and sodden as the bed of an ancient lake after the weeks of rain.' Here we feel the weight of the emphasis on 'sunken', 'deserted', 'shallow bare', 'black and sodden'. When he describes the rain, again we can feel its weight in 'the plastering beat of icy rain on his bare skull'. The same effect is achieved in the description of the attacks by the horse. It is partly because of the solid, concrete world achieved by the language that we are forced in one sense at least to accept the physical reality of the horse.

Consider the following:

1 Briefly list other images from 'The Ice Palace' that help to establish the heat of the South or cold of the North. Are there other words or phrases in the story that seem vivid, which help evoke the atmosphere?

2 Read 'Go Down, Moses'[2] and consider the various references to the heat in the story. Compare the effect of the descriptions in the story with those in 'The Ice Palace'. Which makes most impression on you?

3 Briefly list any other images from 'The Wedge-Tailed Eagle'. Do you feel they add anything to the story?

4 Read 'Shark Fins'[4] – list any images you find, and consider whether they seem appropriate to the story.

5 What strengths do you think there are in Hemingway's style? Do you prefer it to that of writers who use a more descriptive style?

6 Try to write the opening two paragraphs of 'The Ice Palace' in the style of Hemingway.

7 Try to list any further descriptions of the rain or the horse in 'The Rain Horse' that rely on simple but emphatic language. Do such descriptions help to clarify the story in any way?

Symbolism

We have already seen when discussing 'Odour of Chrysanthemums'[1,3] (see 'The Setting') and 'Lie thee down, Oddity'[2] (see 'Man and Nature'), the significance of 'symbol'. The chrysanthemums seem to represent various stages in Elizabeth Bates' marriage; Mr Cronch's hat seems to represent faith or security, attractive to the baby (p. 117) and bringing consolation to the man about to face his death. The use of symbols to help define the point of a story is another element of style that we may frequently meet. Perhaps not surprisingly, we often meet more symbolic writing from poets who also write short stories.

Walter de la Mare's 'The Wharf'[2] relies on the contrast between two symbols, the wharf itself and the midden in the farmyard. While not at first easy to grasp, the story focuses on the reflections of a woman looking back on a nervous breakdown. Although apparently recovered now, she can never lose the impression of the vision – an immense wharf where 'gigantic beings' who might be devils or angels in an 'eternal Present' are depositing a 'foul mess' which she realizes are 'dead souls'. Most terrible to the woman is the 'sublime indifference' with which they undertake the task: they are neither the 'good' nor 'bad' souls, just the ordinary ones. She feels that if life can be reduced to such indifference, then it is entirely futile. She becomes 'lost amid the gloom of her own mind'.

Sent to a farm to 'recover', she is at first suicidal. Gradually however she is led towards a recognition of the more positive elements offered in life. She is led by a heifer 'with ... delicate head and lustrous eyes' to a dungheap, 'a heap of old stable manure' and it is in this unlikely image that she finds the antidote to the wharf. As the farmer explains, the midden symbolizes the completeness of Nature: covered as it is in a profusion of flowers which will decay back into the midden, allowing beauty and 'ugliness' to flourish together, interdependently. The understanding that comes with this allows the woman to come to terms with the horrific image of the wharf, 'turned it outside in, so to speak'.

This is a story that deals with large themes without loading them with undue significance. The story suggests an attitude to life through its use of symbol without seeming heavyhanded. We all wonder at some time, what is the point of life – the two symbols seem to clarify two possible attitudes towards such thoughts.

Consider the following:

1 In what other ways are the positive elements of life presented in the story?

2 Do you find the image of the wharf horrific? What aspects of the description make the most impression?

3 Apparently about a nervous breakdown, with the nightmarish image of the wharf at its centre, and a dungheap as a positive symbol, this seems an unlikely story to claim as a positive statement about life. How might you argue that it is?

Tone of voice

Some writers remember sharply the strength and vigour of the language with which they grew up, recognizing it as a vivid element of their own memories. In writing about their own backgrounds, the way in which the characters speak can reflect not only something of the vitality of a specific personality, but also some of the energy of a whole community. The voice of Alan Sillitoe's main characters tends to be uncompromising, cynical, anti-authority, representative of a class – of the poor, the deprived, the disadvantaged – with whom such characters identify. The main character of V.S. Naipaul's 'The Baker's Story'[4] is struggling to escape a poverty that engulfed many in the Trinidad of that time as well as the problems of race. In his tone however is a good humoured, ironic acceptance of his fate, with an equal capacity to overcome it.

Colin in 'The Loneliness of the Long-Distance Runner'[7] shows his anger and his refusal to submit to authority throughout the story: 'It's a good life I'm saying to myself, if you don't give in to coppers and Borstal-bosses and the rest of them bastard-faced In-laws.' The underlying anger is partly expressed in the vigour of the language, and it would be difficult to reflect such feelings in more polished, elegant phrases.

Sillitoe is often at pains to suggest the difficulties such characters have in expressing themselves, while showing the dignity with which they conduct themselves. In 'The Fishing-Boat Picture'[7], Harry begins his story with an awareness that he can only write the account plainly: 'I'd rather not make what I'm going to write look foolish by using dictionary words.' The possibly autobiographical 'The Decline and Fall of Frankie Buller'[7] ends with a sense that books – and the education that they imply – merely cut you off from your past: 'And I with my books have not seen him since. It was like saying goodbye to a big part of me, for ever.'

'The Baker's Story' also begins with a vivid sense of the personality of the narrator. 'Look at me. Black as the Ace of Spades, and ugly to match.' His resilience also shows through – while born into poverty, he has managed to make money out of a bakery, telling those who ask, 'I does always tell them I make my dough from dough. Ha! You like that one?' Once again, he almost takes pride in a lack of education: 'Well, you hearing me talk, and I don't have to tell you I didn't have no education.' Despite a lack of formal education however, he more than compensates through the sharpness of his intelligence. The story is concerned with the complexity of racial attitudes in the West Indies – between islands and between those who have been settled there. We are given a clear sense of his identity – from Grenada – and of the attitude towards the Grenadians, which is an important element of the story's purpose.

In many of D. H. Lawrences' stories and those of Bill Naughton, we are aware of the same attempt to represent characters who come from poor or deprived areas. They are given the colloquial language of their area necessary to reflect the circumstances of their existence. Lawrence's stories in particular often revolve around relationships between men and women where the woman's desire to express herself in a more creative, fulfilling way begins to founder on the inarticulate nature of the man.

Consider the following:

1 Are you convinced by Sillitoe's characters – do they seem real? By comparing a character from another story whom you feel to be less convincing, try to decide what quality helps to create an impression of reality.

2 What kind of person does the narrator of 'The Baker's Story' seem to be?

3 Read 'Seeing a Beauty Queen Home'[5], or 'The Disgrace of Jim Scarfedale'[7] – how does the personality of the narrator affect the story?

4 Read 'Strike Pay'[3]. Would the story be more or less successful if it was written in reported speech rather than in dialogue?

Character

A writer may influence our response to a story through the way in which he or she describes the characters. At times, the narrator will give us an impression – which may suggest as much about him: as when Dylan's imagination conjures up Uncle Jim as a fox, 'leaning over the wall of the sty with the pig's legs sticking out of his mouth' in 'Peaches'[2]. Leila's excitement in 'Her First Ball'[2] is partly suggested by the way in which the world around her is seen to be dancing, in a series of similes and metaphors, 'past waltzing lampposts', or the quivering jet of gas that couldn't wait: 'It was dancing already.'

The use of such images helps to give us an impression of what the character is like, rather than a purely physical description. In 'The Wharf'[2], the child in her frock is seen 'for all the world like the white petals of a flower: its flashing crimson fruit just peeping out beneath'. Or we can consider the description of the horse like a 'nightmarish leopard', in 'The Rain Horse'[2], which brings with it a sense of the alien presence it seems to the young man.

At times, we are given only an initial glimpse of a character, filled in gradually as we hear his or her voice, or see his or her behaviour. Thus Tarloff, in 'The Dry Rock'[8] is seen only as 'a little grey man', his size and defeated air helping to heighten the moral courage he shows. Harry Bellamy in 'The Ice Palace'[2] is described merely as 'tall, broad and brisk', suggesting something of the size and energy of the North, in contrast to the lethargy of the previous section. We learn that Mr Hinds in 'The Raffle'[4] 'is a big beater', and also of the contradiction in his nature that leads us to the incident at the centre of the story. In some stories, it is an important part of the whole effect that we hear the character, as we do the repeated exclamations of Lacey in 'Samphire'[2], which help us to feel Molly's growing tension more intensely.

Assignments

1 How does Fitzgerald use images and other descriptive phrases to bring out a distinction between the characters we meet from the South and those from the North in 'The Ice Palace'[2]?

2 Compare any two or three stories in which extremes of

climate are an important part of the story's effect. Which author succeeds best in making you feel vividly the conditions he or she describes – why? (Apart from 'The Ice Palace', you might consider 'Go Down, Moses'[2], 'The Rain Horse'[2], 'The Man who Loved Islands'[3] or 'A Drink of Water'[4].)

3 Compare and contrast the way in which 'The Ice Palace' and 'Indian Camp'[2] are written. How does the style in which they are written contribute to your enjoyment of each story?

4 Compare the differences you find in the use of dialogue between 'The Raid'[8], 'The Killers'[9], 'Blackout'[4], and 'Strike Pay'[3] – try to define any differences you find, and try to suggest which you prefer and why.

5 Do you find 'The Wharf'[2] a depressing or positive story? How does the way in which it is written help to guide our response?

6 Compare the personalities of the main characters in 'The Baker's Story'[4], 'Seeing a Beauty Queen Home'[5], and 'The Disgrace of Jim Scarfedale'[7]. How does the way in which each presents himself affect the story?

7 In what various ways are characters described in 'The Dry Rock'[8]? How do we reach our conclusions about the characters? (Description, image, actions, dialogue?)

8 Take any three stories, and try to re-write the opening two or three paragraphs of each in the different style of another author who appeals to you.

9 Write a story which is dependent on the vivid creation of a particular effect of weather. (Like 'The Rain Horse', it could be based on a return to childhood memories, or the weather might represent some negative or positive aspect of your situation.)

10 Try to write an episode from your own childhood in the style of Hemingway.

11 Write a story in which a character is confronted with a choice between two courses of action. Try to represent each choice symbolically.

12 Write a story about a thoroughly unlikeable character. (Think particularly about how you will describe the character – through images, physical details, the sound of his voice, his actions . . .?)

The Novella

In discussions about the short story, the term 'novella' is sometimes used. There is some argument about the origins of the term – it is similar to words used in French, Italian and Spanish to denote tales and short stories. Loosely, it could be said to describe long short stories. Clearly such a definition presents its own problems: what is the difference between a short novel and a long short story?

The novella has more in common with the short story. Usually we are still concerned with Poe's 'single effect', but less reliant on a single instance to show it. The novella may not merely confront us with a single key incident, but a series of significant moments in the life of a character; each of the moments may be governed by a 'unity of effect', but will not reveal the entire nature of the character.

The effect in the novella seems more serious, sometimes tragic, than the usually lighter effect of the short story proper. There seems a greater depth to the novella, where an idea or theme can often support and intensify the development of character.

Being honest to yourself

In authority

In terms of the collections considered here, 'The Secret Sharer'[1] could be defined as a novella. Its single effect revolves around the relationship between Leggatt and the Captain, and reaches its climax when both resolve their predicaments at the end of the story. However, this is a complex tale, an intense psychological study, always close to a tragic conclusion, written in a deliberately enigmatic way. More simply, 'The Loneliness of the Long-Distance Runner'[7] moves between the present situation, and scenes from the central character's past, unified by the distinct tone and style of his speech, to suggest his determination to stay true to himself and his own morality.

The initial setting of Joseph Conrad's 'The Secret Sharer'[1] plunges both reader and the Captain into an unfamiliar world –

lines of fishing stakes in 'a mysterious system ... incomprehensible in its division' at the head of the Gulf of Siam. We learn that the Captain too is a 'stranger to the ship' which reinforces a sense of alienation that is part of the story's effect. As importantly, the Captain feels himself to be 'somewhat of a stranger to myself', concerned to be 'faithful to that ideal conception of one's own personality every man sets up for himself secretly'. We are to be confronted with a stage in the Captain's life where he tries to live up to his own expectations of himself.

There is 'unity of effect' within the story – all the incidents bear upon the 'test' he faces on the ship, and while there is eventually a 'significant moment' at the climax of the story, he has had to face several testing moments by then. The tone of the story is more serious than others considered here, it is the morality of the Captain that is explored; he has chosen the sea as a career because he considers it 'invested with an elementary moral beauty by the absolute straightforwardness of its appeal and by the singleness of its purpose'. Ironically, the moral predicament he will have to face is anything but a clear issue, involving him in the shelter of a murderer, and in helping the murderer to escape.

Perhaps the key moment of the story is when, having determined to take the first watch himself – to the evident surprise of the first and second officer – he catches sight of a dark head in the water, clutching the bottom of the ladder. Once Leggatt is brought on board, making clear that his choice is to sink or board the ship – the Captain feels that he is indeed facing a 'clear issue'. A remarkably close identification between the two is created: 'A mysterious communication was established already between us two.' A series of 'double' or 'twin' images follow, 'followed me like my double on the poop', 'faced by my own reflection in the depth of a sombre and immense mirror', which continue after Leggatt has told his story.

Leggatt presents his crime without conventional guilt. His account seems self-assertive, swinging between shame and pride, guilt and a consciousness of his own right in the case. However, the crime is murder. His own crew mates and captain from the *Sephora* are confident that he should suffer the appropriate penalty: they have reduced it to a 'clear issue'. The captain from the *Sephora* has not the imagination to see the moral complexity of the case. He believes that it is right to exact the due punishment whatever the circumstances.

The Captain cannot see the issue in such clear terms. Leggatt has committed a single act, under provocation, and is unlikely to do so again. It is right that he suffers, but not that he dies. However, the Captain's determination to save Leggatt is not presented as an easy issue either. The most dramatic moment of the story, as he risks the ship to save Leggatt, takes place – symbolically – in the dark. Yet he has shown the courage to confront the complexity of the situation; ultimately, we may argue that he has taken a morally responsible decision. It is not always possible merely to impose a moral framework on each evil act.

The Captain's determination to take the ship as close to land as possible to give Leggatt the best chance of swimming to the shore, becomes a double test, which allows the predicaments of both men to be resolved. Leggatt is saved, though he will always be an outcast – 'it would not do for me to come to life again' – while the Captain's seamanship is proved, if only through the timely mark of the hat he had lent to Leggatt.

From the outside, the Captain's behaviour clearly seems at times bizarre – some of the episodes verge on the humorous, with the Captain's desperate assumption of deafness to protect himself from the probing of the captain of the *Sephora*. However, he also finds the 'clear issue': to save Leggatt, that allows him also to confirm his own expectations of himself.

The story remains enigmatic at times then, true to its initial mention of 'a mysterious system ... incomprehensible in its division' – a suggestiveness that we so often find in the short story. However we discuss the story, it seems unlikely that we can reduce it to an easy interpretation, any more than Leggatt's fate is an easy issue. There is a depth to it, an intensity, that is not always true of other short stories.

Consider the following:

1 Why do you think that there is such a close identification between the two men?

2 By looking closely at the response of the other crew members towards the Captain, and the impression he makes on the captain of the *Sephora*, how do you think he is regarded?

3 Is the Captain right to protect Leggatt? Why do you think he

does so? (Compare his response to that of Bolton towards Jackson in 'Late Night on Watling Street'.)

4 Do you have any sympathy with the first mate or the captain of the *Sephora*? Are their views towards Leggatt right?

5 Briefly list the differences in the story had it been written in the third person (i) by another character on the ship (ii) by a narrator outside the action entirely who knows everything about the characters.

6 Do you think there are many differences between 'The Secret Sharer' and an ordinary short story? If so, list them.

7 Read two other works by Conrad, 'The Shadow Line' and 'Typhoon' – do you find any similarities between these and 'The Secret Sharer'?

Against authority

Alan Sillitoe's 'The Loneliness of the Long-Distance Runner'[7] might also be claimed as a novella. Colin, the main character through whose eyes we see the story develop, shares some qualities with the Captain in 'The Secret Sharer'. Like the Captain, Colin wants to live up to his own expectations of himself, but he too is capable of seeing the complexity of moral judgements. He identifies with a quite different code of conduct from those who run the Borstal in which he is imprisoned, or indeed from those whom he believes run society.

His understanding of 'honesty' is less to do with obeying the law, than in being honest to himself: 'Because another thing people like the governor will never understand is that I *am* honest ... I think my honesty is the only sort in the world ...' Like many of Sillitoe's heroes, Colin has nothing in common with middle-class values, or with those who are prepared to struggle decently for a comfortable existence. He identifies with people whom he feels are undermined by those with education or power, 'the cops, governors, posh whores, penpushers, army officers, Members of Parliament', all of whom he would line up against a wall and shoot. He sees himself as already 'in a war of my own, that I was born into one ...' quite separate from 'Government wars ... they've got nowt to do with me'.

The story is about the determined way in which he sets about demonstrating his honesty. But it is less to do with seeing a character at a crucial point of his life, than with seeing an attitude to life characterized in a single personality. We are given a more intense view of Colin, in more depth than we might in a story of only one key moment. The structure of the story does eventually focus on a significant moment, but it is an anticipated climax, and merely bears out the strength of character that the story presents us with. Other sections of the story add the depth by suggesting something of the life Colin lives, his criminality, the reasons for his rejection of society.

Sillitoe tells the story in Colin's own words, in the first person. The style suggests Colin's lack of education, is colloquial, and often in long sentences as we follow his often breathless thoughts. He is training hard for the 'Borstal Blue Ribbon Prize Cup for Long Distance Cross Country Running (All England)', the pomposity of its title contributing to Colin's judgement of its value. As far as the governor is concerned, by giving Colin privileges and the opportunity to win the cup, he is helping to reform him, to make him a decent citizen. As far as Colin is concerned, he will take the privileges, but to win the cup would be a form of collaboration which he rejects entirely.

The whole focus of Colin's thoughts is on disappointing the governor's expectations in as obvious a way as possible. He is a good runner, trains hard and would win the race, but it is not why he does it. He appreciates the freedom his early morning training brings him, 'sometimes I think that I've never been so free as during that couple of hours when I'm trotting up the path out of the gates ...', free to think, and free from the demands of others.

The second section of the story is almost a short story in itself – an account of the crime for which he was arrested, and of his family life. Cynical and self-satisfied, convinced of the stupidity of the police, the 'twist' of this 'story' is that he gets caught at all. What this section does do though, is to deepen our image of Colin, helping to explain why he has become as he has. It makes clear his working-class background, and some sense of its deprivations and lack of scope.

The final section takes up the race itself, a confirmation of Colin's determination to win in his own way. He feels that he has been born into a position in society in which he is bound to lose – the final paragraph makes clear that he is back in prison. He can, however, make a gesture of heroic defiance, of solidarity with his own class, of integrity.

His telling of the story is grimly humorous, but we may feel eventually saddened by the story. While we may not admire the morality Colin feels is represented in the governor, and his 'class', we may feel something is lost in the waste of Colin's energy and courage.

Consider the following:

1 Do you think Colin was right to lose the race in such an obvious way? Do you feel admiration or contempt for him?

2 What do you think his gesture has achieved?

3 Do you think that Colin is unfair when he talks of the governor and his class?

4 What differences can you find in the way the story is structured from that of other stories you have read? (Is it based around a single moment? Is it based around a turning point in a character's life? To what extent does it 'tell a story'?)

5 Is there any point to the middle section (II) of the story? Or does it merely get in the way of the story – of what happens – in the first and last sections?

6 Why do you think it was written in the first person rather than the third person?

7 How important is the style in which this story is written? (Compare it with 'Her First Ball'[2] for instance – how do the different styles tell us more about the characters?)

8 Do you find the story funny in any way? Try to explain why if you do – using details from the story.

Assignments

1 Write the story of 'The Secret Sharer' from the point of view of either the chief mate or the captain of the *Sephora*. (What would the focus of your story become? Would there be a key

moment? Would the setting be of interest? What would need to be lost in Conrad's story?)

2 Write the governor's report on Colin Smith, based on what he would know of him, as he leaves Borstal.

3 Both the Captain and Colin Smith want to live up to their own expectations of themselves. Do you believe they succeed? Do you have admiration for either, or for one more than the other? Try to explain your reasons.

4 Discuss 'honesty' from the point of view of any three of the following: the Captain, Leggatt, the captain of the *Sephora*, Colin Smith, the governor.

5 How important is 'the story' – what actually happens – in either 'The Secret Sharer' or 'The Loneliness of the Long-Distance Runner'? (Look closely at incidents which increase the tension or our involvement in the story; what other focus of interest is there?)

6 Compare which seems to you the 'key moment' of each story. How is the reader's interest maintained? How well has the moment been prepared or anticipated earlier in the story? Which seems the more successful?

7 Look closely at the setting of each story. Which is most important to the story? Which makes the most impression on you?

8 Write a story in which the main character is isolated, unsure of her/himself, but determined to prove her/himself. (Consider the setting, whether it is to be written in first or third person, whether there will be a series of moments, or a key moment . . .)

9 Write a story in which a woman makes a defiant gesture against a system that expects her to live in a certain way.

Conclusion

The stories considered here have been taken from the GCSE Boards' suggested reading. There are many other collections available that consider other stories. One of the strengths of using the short story in English or English Literature coursework folders is that you can follow your own reading tastes. The GCSE approach positively encourages such independent reading.

It is not difficult to adapt your own assignments from others that you find here. Chapter headings give some idea of the themes often found within the short story. Headings and subheadings within each chapter suggest more specific approaches. Other ideas often cut across neat chapter divisions. Two ideas we meet often in these stories concern the effect on people of education or of death.

'Cane is Bitter'[4] most clearly dramatizes the conflict between generations that education can introduce. The older generation of a simple community can glimpse the opportunities education may bring. They cannot conceive how dramatically the fruits of education can change the young: that the safety and attractions of a traditional culture can quickly seem confining once the possibilities beyond it have been grasped.

Education can divide relationships too. In 'The Red Ball'[4], Bolan's father partly resents the educational opportunities open to his son, always denied to him. In 'Daughters of the Vicar'[3], we see how being educated in an inappropriate way can cut individuals off from the community; in Louisa's case, ultimately from her family as well. The opportunities or consequences of education then are often offered as a cause of tension or conflict at the centre of a story.

Death too can provide the central incident in the exploration of character. We may question what we die for – as Tengar does at the end of 'Hunters and Hunted'[4]. It may be in the reactions to death that the nature of a personality is revealed. Those reactions may lay bare a whole life – as they do in 'Daughters of the Late Colonel'[1] – or may suggest childhood innocence, in 'Indian Camp'[2] for example, or growing awareness of the reality of death as is revealed in 'The Living'[8]. We all have to come to terms with death. We can be helped to do so by comparing the responses of fiction.

While the 'theme' of a story might be a helpful starting point in considering its effect, it is the other features that usually influence our response to it. To enjoy reading a short story is important. To determine *why* we enjoy it is equally important in any critical process. Try to account for your reactions to any short story you are reading. What do you consider its most striking feature? Do you identify closely with one of the characters? Do you like the way in which it is written – its simplicity, or the way ideas are clarified through symbols or images? Do you enjoy the setting of the story? Are you amused by it? Does it puzzle or surprise you – particularly in its conclusion?

At times, of course, you will dislike a short story, sometimes strongly. Has it disturbed or distressed you? Do you feel the story-line seems inappropriate? Is there something in your response that tells you more about yourself? A short story is uncompromising – it merely offers itself. We cannot change it to conform with our own view of the world. It may well challenge us as individuals and make us consider our own feelings and ideas.

Try to read as widely as possible. Where you have enjoyed an author of any of the stories considered here, or one that you have discovered from your own reading, seek out further stories that he or she has written. Many of the writers discussed in this guide have published anthologies of their own short stories. It is only through wide reading that you can develop your own taste, and begin to understand it.

Read carefully too. An initial reading is usually for enjoyment – you may well become immersed in the narrative itself. Check back on further readings however for the reasons for your reaction – whether positive or negative. Try to find the details in the writing that have led to your response – the occasional amusing phrase, the striking descriptive detail, the use of dialogue, the unexpected ending, the horrific moment that has distressed you.

A wide range of assignments has been offered at the end of each chapter. In many cases, you could also adapt or simply use ideas from the 'Consider the following' sections on each story. Don't rush the writing. Whatever your first impressions about a story, they may well change. Note down your feelings. Make

Conclusion

further notes in rereading the story. Test your ideas on others – discuss the stories with friends and with your teacher. Have you perhaps misunderstood a detail? Do others see the story differently – and why? Only then should you begin to plan your written work. Writing about Literature – either critically or imaginatively – can be stimulating, creative and enjoyable. You may learn more about yourself, your feelings, and of others around you.

Read widely then; enjoy your reading but think about it too. Develop your own ideas and your own taste in short stories. Don't dismiss stories you do not immediately like. Talk about them with others. Do some people enjoy them? Why? Thinking about stories can help to develop your own ideas, your own independence, and is always a positive and fulfilling activity.

General questions

1 By considering carefully the personality of each child, write part of 'The Little Pet'[8], or 'Message from the Pig-Man'[8], or 'The Red Ball'[4] in the first person. Concentrate on one or two incidents. Write about 400 words. (If you prefer, write about 200 words each on *two* of these stories.)

2 Consider *three* stories discussed in the chapter 'Parents and Children', or any you have read that deal with the relationship between parents and children. Write about your attitudes towards the relationship. (Consider from whose viewpoint the story is shown, and with whom you have the most sympathy.)

3 Having read 'The Ice Palace'[2], discuss Sally-Carroll's distinction between 'canine' and 'feline'. Use her definitions to write about characters from at least *three* other stories. Do you think that the terms require any qualification?

4 Consider any *three* stories discussed in the chapter 'A Significant Experience', or from your own reading. Write about any characters that have faced a 'turning point' in their lives. What were the consequences of their actions? Did each character deserve his or her fate?

5 Referring to at least *three* stories about people who are isolated, or outside society in some way, write about your feelings towards each character. Is it easy to feel sympathetic towards them, or is your reaction mixed with dislike or distrust? Would your reaction be similar in real life?

6 'Samphire'[2], 'Daughters of the Late Colonel'[1] and 'The Killers'[9] all rely to a great extent on dialogue. Compare the use of dialogue in each and any similarities or differences that emerge *or* (i) Write about 300–400 words of one of these stories as a drama script for a radio production *and* (ii) Write a further couple of paragraphs (about 150 words) about what you feel is lost or gained by your approach.

7 Read 'Lie thee down, Oddity'[2]. Write a front page story, as if for a tabloid newspaper, of Mr Cronch's death, and his actions since leaving his job as a gardener. Add to this a brief leading article with the paper's judgement of his behaviour.

8 Compare any one or two stories discussed in the chapter 'The Setting', and any *two* from your own reading. Write about the different ways in which writers achieve a particular setting – and discuss which you prefer *or* Take any *two* stories from your own reading which introduce a setting unfamiliar to you. Explain how you feel the writer has tried to establish a particular sense of place, and suggest how successfully you think he or she has achieved his or her effect.

9 Referring to at least three stories discussed in the chapter 'Humanity and Nature' or from your own reading, write about the attitude humanity takes towards the natural world. (Do the characters seem to show respect/admiration for the natural world? What does this attitude amount to? What are your feelings towards their actions?)

10 By comparing any two stories from your own reading with any discussed in the chapter on 'Humour', try to define your own sense of humour, suggesting what you do find amusing, and what you do not.

11 By comparing any two stories from your own reading with one or two of those discussed in the chapter 'Style', write about the ways in which writers use language in their stories. Explain your own preference *or* Compare three stories by American writers, 'Go Down, Moses'[2], 'The Raid'[8], and 'Indian Camp'[2]. What similarities and differences do you find in the respective style of each? (You will need to look closely here at words, phrases, description, imagery, etc.)

12 Compare the tone of the narrator's voice in 'The Loneliness of the Long-Distance Runner'[7], or 'On Saturday Afternoon'[7] with that of Sprake in 'Shot Actress – Full Story'[8] or the narrator of 'The Baker's Story'[4]. What do we learn of the narrators from the way in which each expresses himself?

13 By comparing two or three stories, discuss whether what happens in the story, and the nature of whatever is revealed, is affected by the sex or race of the main character.

Questions for wider reading

1 Write about at least *three* stories in which the title is an important element of the story's significance.

2 By considering *three or four* stories, show how the opening sentence of each helps to clarify the point of the story.

3 By comparing *two or three* stories show how some stories depend on a 'key moment', whilst others suggest a character through a series of episodes.

4 Take two stories written in the third person and rewrite the opening page in the first person. (Who will be the central character? Is it obvious or will a lesser character have to observe what happens?) *or* Take two stories written in the first person and rewrite the opening page in the third person. (From 'outside' the story, or as a character within it?) *and* Write two or three paragraphs suggesting the kind of differences that have emerged from the rewriting.

5 Compare one or two stories that depend on symbolism or the use of imagery to make their effect, with one or two that are simply written. Which style do you prefer and why?

6 Compare any two stories that had a strong effect on you in different ways (for example you may have found a story particularly moving or amusing, tragic or pointless, or just complicated or unsettling).

7 Write about two characters who have made a strong impression on you (for example you may have closely identified with their experience, a character may make you angry or sad, feel contempt or admiration).

8 Take any dramatic 'key moment' from a story, and present it as a news story in either a local or tabloid paper.

Questions for wider reading

9 Rewrite the ending of a story you have read, trying to maintain the style of the writer, *and* Write two or three paragraphs explaining why you made the change, and whether you feel it was successful.

10 Try to present a significant moment from a story as a play script for a radio production.

Index of stories discussed in the text

From Collection 1

The Lumber Room, 5, 75–6, 77, 78
The Daughters of the Late Colonel, 7, 46–8, 50–1, 95, 98
The Secret Sharer, 88–91, 93–4
Odour of Chrysanthemums, 9, 54, 55–7, 82

From Collection 2

The Ice Palace, 4, 24–8, 55, 59–60, 80, 86, 98
Her First Ball, 4, 7, 86
The Road, 6, 9, 34–9
The Wedge-Tailed Eagle, 7, 63–8, 70, 80, 82
Lie thee down, Oddity, 6, 68–71, 82, 98
The Peaches, 7, 55, 58–9, 61–2, 86
The Secret Life of Walter Mitty, 7, 39, 72–3, 78
The Rain Horse, 8, 65–7, 70, 71, 81, 82, 86, 87
Samphire, 10, 48–51, 72, 86, 98
Growing Up, 22, 28, 71
Her First Ball, 24–8
Indian Camp, 28–32, 52–4, 80, 81, 82, 87, 95, 99
Go Down, Moses, 82, 87, 99
The Wharf, 83–4, 86

From Collection 3

Odour of Chrysanthemums, 9, 54, 55–7, 82
Daughters of the Vicar, 51, 95

From Collection 4

A Village Tragedy, 5, 9
Hunters and Hunted, 7, 9, 28–32, 54, 63–8, 70, 95
Cane is Bitter, 7, 39, 55, 60–1, 95
Black-out, 9
The Red Ball, 11, 14–15, 95, 98
The Enemy, 17, 19–21, 22

Drunkard of the River, 33
Shark Fins, 82
The Baker's Story, 84–5, 99

From Collection 5

Late Night on Watling Street, 8, 34, 39–42
The Key of the Cabinet, 22, 77
Poison Pincher, 77
Seeing a Beauty Queen Home, 85, 87

From Collection 6

My Oedipus Complex, 6, 7, 22, 61, 73–4, 76, 78

From Collection 7

On Saturday Afternoon, 33, 76–9, 99
The Destructors, 42–5
The Loneliness of the Long-Distance Runner, 84–5, 88, 91–4, 99
The Fishing-Boat Picture, 84
The Decline and Fall of Frankie Buller, 84
The Disgrace of Jim Scarfedale, 85, 87

From Collection 8

Shot Actress – Full Story, 4, 8
The Dry Rock, 5, 9, 86, 87
Uncle Ernest, 6, 34–9
The Little Pet, 7, 11, 12–14, 21, 98
A Present for a Good Girl, 9
The Raid, 9, 54, 55, 57–8, 61, 87, 99
The Living, 15, 22, 28, 33, 54, 95
Through the Tunnel, 15–16
A Message from the Pig-Man, 17–19, 21, 22, 98
The First Seven Years, 22
Life of Ma Parker, 54

From Collection 9

The Necklace, 1
The Killers, 6, 52–4, 61, 87, 98